SECRETS OF

Surveillance

SECRETS OF

Surveillance

A Professional's Guide to Tailing Subjects by Vehicle, Foot, Airplane, and Public Transportation

ACM IV Security Services

Paladin Press • Boulder, Colorado

WARNING

Laws governing the investigative techniques vary from state to state. Before undertaking any potentially illegal activity, check with the appropriate law enforcement agencies.

Also by ACM IV Security Services:

Surveillance Countermeasures:
   a Serious Guide to Detecting, Evading,
   and Eluding Threats to Personal Privacy

Secrets of Surveillance: A Professional's Guide to Tailing Subjects by Vehicle, Airplane, and Public Transportation
by ACM IV Security Services

Copyright 1993 by ACM IV Security Services

ISBN 0-87364-722-X
Printed in the United States of America

Published by Paladin Press, a division of
Paladin Enterprises, Inc., P.O. Box 1307,
Boulder, Colorado 80306, USA.
(303) 443-7250

Direct inquiries and/or orders to the above address.

CONTENTS

PREFACE

The art of physical surveillance is as ageless as one person's curiosity to determine the activities of another. This art has progressed from the simple act of eavesdropping to a sophisticated practice requiring much expertise.

The modern art of physical surveillance has evolved into a virtual science through the time-tested methods developed by the intelligence and security agencies of many countries. These methods of employment are not unique to the shadow warriors of countries such as the United States, Britain, Israel, or the former Soviet Union. They are, in fact, a compilation of skills that have been developed through many years of counterespionage and criminal investigative efforts. This proven tradecraft has grown common to the most professional practitioners.

Surveillance of the future promises many possibilities. The day will emerge in which surveillance operators will use computers rather than maps. Miniature computers will be used in surveillance vehicles to receive initial grid coordinate entries from specialized sensors and to relay this information to satellite platforms.

The satellites will immediately transmit a city map image projecting the exact position of the vehicle being followed to each vehicle on the surveillance team. The drivers of surveillance vehicles will wear specialized glasses with the capability to send visual impulse signals to concealed video and photography equipment, capable of recording images through a fiber-optic lens in the vehicles' antennas. Surveillance operators on foot will wear superminiature concealed body communications equipment—voice-activated, of course. The undetectable transmissions-receiving earpiece will also contain a bionic listening capability. Surveillance operators will wear contact lenses with an enhanced night-vision capability. They will also carry palm-sized devices with the capability to project holographic images of people or structures to distract or deceive the individual under surveillance.

This futuristic vision of surveillance is neither complete nor contrived. In fact, the resources available to surveillance professionals today would confound the novice. Despite the gadgetry referenced, note that each equipment application described in the previous scenario of "surveillance to come" involved the surveillance operator. This is important, because from the beginning of its existence throughout the foreseeable future, surveillance depends on the human element for execution. Individuals skilled in the art of physical surveillance are essential to its effectiveness. In fact, the majority of people in the investigative community currently practicing the art are restricted to conducting surveillance the "old-fashioned way" because of resource constraints.

This book is directed to the true practitioner of surveillance: the individual who seeks the in-depth knowledge necessary to develop the complex skills required of a professional operator. Virtually all available literature that addresses the art of physical surveillance provides little insight regarding the skills and tactics involved. These publications—under the purview of surveillance manuals—concentrate heavily on the employment of technical surveillance devices while rehashing the same basic or antiquated tactics of the most integral aspect of any surveillance operation: physical surveillance.

This is not to say that technical surveillance is not a significant aspect of a comprehensive surveillance effort. In fact, this book will address how technical capabilities can be employed to support a surveillance operation. But an overreliance on technical surveillance will significantly limit the success of any agency involved in surveillance operations. Listening devices can provide invaluable information in specific situations, and beaconing devices are effective in monitoring the general travels of a suspect individual. Despite these factors, physical surveillance is the only method that provides the capability to develop information regarding an individual's illegal or operational activities wherever they occur.

While sufficient information regarding technical surveillance and its applications is readily available, this is not the case with physical surveillance. The true art of surveillance cannot be sufficiently documented through subject research and peripheral knowledge. To develop the art, one must study from those few who have stalked the streets and stood in the shadows.

A surveillance operation can be conducted from one extreme of detail to the other. This book instructs to the extreme of a fully integrated, systematic effort employed for extended periods of time with absolute discretion. Granted, the requirements of many readers may not reach this extreme, but the information herein will satisfy the objectives of surveillance at any point along the operational continuum. Although the degree of sophistication detailed in this book may not be necessary for many surveillance operations, any individuals with the expertise to operate at the extreme of sophistication can certainly adapt to any operational requirement. For instance, a surveillance team may not be required to approach the surveillance of an unfaithful husband with the same degree of sophistication as would be necessary against a terrorist, but any team that approaches an operation against a terrorist in the same manner as it would an unfaithful husband will certainly be compromised and very possibly killed. This analogy applies in varying degrees to espionage agents, drug dealers, and any other type of violent criminal.

Absolute discretion to the extreme that is detailed in this book may not always be necessary, given the nature of the individual under surveillance, but the success of any surveillance operation hinges on the team's ability to remain invisible. Many investigations are conducted for months and even years before enough information is developed to warrant a surveillance of the suspect. In fact, surveillance is normally employed after an investigation has matured to the point at which all investigative leads have been expended without developing the necessary evidence. Surveillance at this point is the investigative tool that is exercised to develop the missing pieces of information that pure investigative research was unable to uncover.

One error on the part of a surveillance team can compromise the entire investigation to the suspect and eradicate all of the previous investigative efforts. Any espionage agent, terrorist, drug dealer, or general criminal who learns that he is under investigation will escape to refuge or alter his activities to thwart any further investigative efforts. Extreme discretion is also necessary because many criminals, to include terrorists and drug dealers, become both confrontational and lethal when surveillance is identified.

Most individuals may be confident that there is no possibility that they could be followed on a 24-hour basis for a period ranging from months to years, having their most intimate secrets and conversations compromised without any indication. There are a number of spies, terrorists, and general criminals in prison today who now know the truth. This book offers the tactical knowledge required for such an effort. It is presented in a straightforward and scientific manner, with no anecdotes or flashy fillers. The intent is to provide the reader with the skills necessary to effectively engage in the most complex discipline of the investigative profession. These pages offer real-world methodology derived through years of experience in many of the intelligence community's most sensitive counterespionage and counterterrorism surveillance operations.

SURVEILLANCE OPERATIONS OVERVIEW

This book provides a comprehensive explanation of surveillance operations and tactics. It is presented in a manner that allows the reader to build understanding based on the developmental detailing of surveillance concepts and their applications. Even a presentation that builds from the most basic tactics to more advanced applications may be difficult to comprehend fully without a general understanding of the overall surveillance methodology. Many of the issues discussed in this overview will be addressed in detail in subsequent chapters. Despite the duplication noted, it is necessary to begin with a basic understanding of how the individual tactics built upon in this book apply to the overall surveillance effort.

TERMINOLOGY

Because of the technical nature of surveillance operations, much of the terminology is unique to the profession. This book limits the terminology to specific issues rather than the street slang that is characteristic of general practitioners.

There are many uncertainties involved in a surveillance operation. In fact, one of the primary purposes of a surveillance is to minimize uncertainty regarding the activities of a target individual. One of the few constants of surveillance is the fact that there will be a target. A *target* is an individual who is the primary focus of a surveillance operation, the purpose of which is to develop information regarding that individual. Throughout this book, the individual who is the focus of the surveillance will be referred to as the target. The vehicle in which the target is travelling, either as the driver or a passenger, will be referred to as the *target vehicle*. When the context of the discussion implies that the tactics addressed are centered around a vehicular surveillance, the target vehicle may also be referred to as simply the target for brevity purposes.

This book addresses the surveillance tactics that are employed in a total surveillance team effort. Throughout this book the surveillance effort will be referred to as a *surveillance team*. An optimally effective surveillance team will normally consist of 12 individuals and six vehicles. This number may increase in some circumstances or may not be necessary in others. The reader who does not have access to these resources should not be discouraged by the numbers. In the first place, any individual who possesses the skills and knowledge to operate at the highest level will certainly be able to tailor this expertise to any level of surveillance. Furthermore, a surveillance professional must be capable of integrating with other surveillance professionals at any level.

A surveillance team consists of surveillants travelling by foot, vehicle, or a combination of both. Throughout this book, a vehicle used by the surveillance team during the course of a surveillance operation will be referred to as a *surveillance vehicle*. When the context of the discussion implies that the vehicle addressed is a surveillance vehicle, it may be referred to as simply a vehicle for brevity purposes. Surveillance vehicles will normally be given a name or designation for identification and radio brevity purposes during the course of an operation. The surveillance vehicles referred to in the operational examples in this book will have phonetic alphabet designators such as Alpha, Bravo, and Charlie.

Individual team members will be referred to as *operators*. They will be further identified as *foot operators* when engaged in foot surveillance. When the context of the discussion implies that the operator is on foot, he will be referred to as simply an operator for brevity purposes. During discussions of vehicular surveillance, there will be references to actions that the surveillance vehicles make, such as transmitting information over the radio. Obviously the surveillance vehicle is not capable of independent thought and action. Again, this is for brevity purposes, and simply implies that an operator inside the surveillance vehicle is taking that action.

Surveillance targets come in all shapes, sizes, and sexes. A well-rounded surveillance team will consist of a good mix of both male and female operators. In fact, some the most capable surveillance operators and most cunning targets are female. During the course of this book, however, the target and surveillance operators will be referred to as he, for brevity purposes only.

When a surveillance operator has visual observation of the target, he is said to have *command* of the target. The term command will be used in this context throughout this book. The primary purpose of a surveillance operation is to develop information regarding a specific target. Depending on the objectives of the operation, the team will be interested in activities that are categorized as either *illegal* or *operational*. These are terms that will be used throughout the book.

Illegal activity is any action that is against the law. Operational activity is any act that is of operational interest to the team or significant in regard to the objectives of the operation. For example, if the objective of an operation is to develop information regarding a target's alleged drug dealings, the fact that he travels frequently to South America is not illegal, but it is certainly of operational interest. The difference between illegal and operational activity is also made because some illegal activities on the part of the target may be of no interest to the surveillance team. It is common for a surveillance team to observe illegal activity that does not support the objectives of the operation and is therefore disregarded in the final evaluation.

SURVEILLANCE DEFINITION AND PRINCIPLES

Physical surveillance is the systematic, discreet observation of an individual to develop information regarding his activities. The operative terms are *systematic, discreet,* and *develop information.*

Surveillance Is Systematic

A professionally and effectively conducted surveillance is orchestrated in a systematic manner. This is accomplished by employing tactics, as a team or individually, that will facilitate effective and discreet surveillance coverage of a target. The majority of this book is dedicated to surveillance tactics.

Surveillance Is Discreet

A surveillance operation can only be effective if it goes undetected by the target or third persons. When a target detects or suspects surveillance, he will take actions to elude or alter his activities to thwart the surveillance effort. Much of a surveillance operation's success centers around the surveillance team's ability to determine behavioral patterns of the target. A target who is aware of the fact that he is under observation can use this knowledge against those who wish to gain insight regarding his activities. By undertaking actions that project a distorted impression of his true patterns, the witting target can frustrate the overall investigative effort by staging fruitless leads to be pursued, thus resulting in wasted time and resources with little justification to continue the operation. In any case, a suspicious or surveillance-conscious target is extremely difficult to cover and exploit.

A surveillance effort must be conducted in a discreet manner through the systematic application of operational tactics. This effort must blend with the surrounding environment to appear natural to the target or third persons.

Third persons, either in the form of the local populace or indigenous security forces, are always considered unreliable, if not hostile, and pose a significant threat to the security of any surveillance effort. For this reason, a surveillance team must blend in at all times—not only when in sight of the target. More sophisticated targets may employ *surveillance detection* or *countersurveillance* to determine the presence of surveillance.

Surveillance detection consists of efforts made by the target to identify the presence of surveillance. Surveillance detection is conducted by one of three methods, or any combination of the three. The three methods are passive, active, and technical surveillance detection.

Passive detection involves the target doing nothing more than observing his surroundings. The target will simply watch for suspicious activity by surrounding vehicles and pedestrians that is possibly indicative of surveillance. Active surveillance detection involves the target making specific, usually preplanned maneuvers to elicit conspicuous reactions from a surveillance effort. By making a surveillance detection maneuver, the target attempts to force members of the surveillance team to react in a manner that allows him to isolate and identify surveillance. Technical surveillance detection involves the use of electronic equipment. The most common methods of technical detection are the use of devices such as frequency scanners or spectrum analyzers to detect radio transmissions or technical monitoring devices that may be indicative of surveillance coverage.

Countersurveillance is the use of an individual or individuals other than the target to detect the presence of surveillance of a target. With countersurveillance coverage, the target does not have to observe his surroundings to identify the presence of surveillance, as is the case with surveillance detection. Countersurveillance operators will be well hidden or disguised as they observe the target's surroundings. Countersurveillance coverage will normally be established around a planned surveillance detection route that the target will travel. The route will incorporate certain maneuvers or take advantage of physical structures that will enable the countersurveillance to isolate and identify the surveillance coverage.

Surveillance detection and countersurveillance are two of the three methods of surveillance countermeasures. The third method is *antisurveillance*. This involves actions taken by the target to evade an identified or suspected surveillance.

Surveillance Is Conducted to Develop Information

The primary objective of virtually any surveillance operation is to develop and collect information regarding the activities of a specified target. Surveillance is employed to identify and document significant activities that satisfy the objectives of the operation. The development of information through surveillance is a progressive and often lengthy process. It is always essential to document thoroughly all observations of the target's activities regardless of how insignificant they may appear to be at the time.

Subsequent observations may occur that provide greater insight to previously documented activities. Through many pieces of information, an overall picture of the target's behavioral patterns is developed. Thorough documentation is critical to surveillance operations in which observations may be presented as judicial evidence. This requires that all documentation be specific as to the time and date that the activities were observed, as well as the name of the individual surveillance operator making those observations.

A surveillance operation will normally begin with limited information regarding the target's activities. It may begin by developing information in order to identify those times or activities on which to concentrate the surveillance effort. As information is developed, target-pattern analysis is conducted to determine patterns that can be exploited by the surveillance team to more effectively anticipate the target's actions. This also enables the surveillance team to determine those times and activities that may be significant in satisfying the objectives of the operation—as opposed to those that are routine and insignificant. Through such target-pattern analysis, a surveillance team can efficiently cover a target by concentrating on those times and activities with the highest potential payoff. This also serves to limit the amount of time that surveillance operators and vehicles may possibly be exposed to the target.

TYPES AND METHODS OF SURVEILLANCE

There are two primary types of physical surveillance—fixed and mobile. *Fixed surveillance* consists of a static position that is established to observe the target's activities at a specified location. Such operations will only satisfy specific objectives because they provide limited insight regarding the target's overall activities. Fixed-surveillance operations are normally conducted when it is suspected that the target will conduct significant activities at a specific location. Such locations may include the target's residence, workplace, an establishment that he frequents, or the residence of an associate. Fixed positions will normally be manned by surveillance operators or monitored through remote video equipment. A surveillance team may use any number of fixed positions during a fixed-surveillance operation. One common use of fixed surveillance is to establish static positions along a designated route to confirm the target's direction of travel. Many fixed-surveillance operations will use an established observation post (which is discussed further in Chapter 5).

Mobile-surveillance operations observe the activities of the target while traveling. Of course, this requires that surveillance operators and vehicles move with the target. Mobile-surveillance operations are conducted either by foot, vehicle, or a combination of both. They are employed to satisfy the objectives of any physical surveillance that cannot be accomplished through a fixed operation. Mobile and fixed surveillance may be used concurrently to enhance the effectiveness of an operation. Fixed-observation posts are frequently employed to support mobile surveillance operations. This book primarily addresses mobile surveillance operations to include the use of fixed positions in support.

There are four primary methods of physical surveillance: 1) foot surveillance, 2) vehicular surveillance, 3) combined foot and vehicular surveillance, and 4) progressive surveillance. The first three of these methods comprise mobile surveillance. Progressive surveillance is conducted through the use of mobile surveillance, fixed surveillance, or a combination of the two.

Foot surveillance operations are conducted to determine the target's activities while travelling by foot. Such operations are normally conducted to achieve limited objectives. Foot surveillance is most effective when there is specific information to indicate that the target will conduct significant activities in an anticipated area while on the ground. This allows the team to concentrate its operators on the ground rather than divide assets between foot and vehicular operators.

Vehicular-surveillance operations determine the target's activities while travelling by vehicle. These operations are normally conducted to determine the target's general travel patterns rather than to develop specific information. Vehicular surveillance is effective when employed at the outset of an operation to develop information for target-pattern analysis while minimizing the initial exposure of operators to the target.

Combined foot- and vehicular-surveillance operations represent the comprehensive employment of all surveillance disciplines. These operations are conducted to observe all the target's activities during a specified period. Combined operations require that the entire team possess a high degree of tactical and technical expertise to ensure an effective transition between vehicular surveillance and foot surveillance. Obviously, such operations increase the exposure of the team's operators and vehicles to the target. Long-term operations will normally require that surveillance operators and vehicles be replaced throughout in order to maintain the security of the operation.

Progressive surveillance is the phased coverage of a target to determine a specific travel pattern. This consists of the surveillance team covering the target from point A to point B and then terminating that phase of the surveillance. The next phase of the operation consists of the surveillance team covering the target from point B to point C and then ending that leg of the operation. This phased coverage continues until a particular travel pattern is determined. Progressive operations can only satisfy very limited objectives and are normally conducted when the surveillance team possesses limited resources or security is the highest priority. The most notorious practitioners of progressive surveillance are terrorist organizations. Such coverage allows the terrorist element to securely determine a specific travel pattern of a potential victim and to identify a point along that route that is suitable for an attack.

Phases of a Mobile-Surveillance Operation

A mobile-surveillance operation is a fluid sequence of tactical maneuvers that are dictated primarily by the actions of the target. This is not to say that the target has any advantage against a professional surveillance effort. In order to cover the target effectively, the team must maintain synchronization through a phased operation with a unity of tactical discipline and purpose.

A comprehensive surveillance operation is conducted in four phases: 1) stakeout, 2) pickup, 3) follow, and 4) box. A surveillance operation will progress through these phases based on the actions of the target. Ideally, an operation will progress through the first four phases and then shift phases in reaction to the target's activities.

The *stakeout* is the positioning of surveillance vehicles or operators, based on the concept of how the team intends to establish initial command of the target. This involves the logical coverage of a specified area to ensure that when the target appears in that area, the team will be able make a smooth and effective transition from static positions to a mobile-surveillance follow. This is accomplished primarily by the use of a boxing method that is intended to cover all routes of travel into and out of the specified area.

The *pickup* occurs when the surveillance team establishes initial command of the target. It is the result of a successful stakeout or surveillance box.

The *follow* encompasses all aspects of the surveillance operation that occur while the target is under command. The follow begins immediately after the pickup.

The *box* phase begins as the target stops during a surveillance follow. As with the stakeout box, a standard surveillance box is a logical positioning of surveillance vehicles or operators to cover all routes of travel out of a specified area. The primary difference between the two types of boxes is that with the standard surveillance box, there is a degree of command over the target because the surveillance team is certain that the target is positioned somewhere within the box.

TYPES OF SURVEILLANCE TARGETS

There is no standard profile of the surveillance target. Targets can range from dumb to deadly. There are, however, general categories in which they can be classified so as to better determine how the team will cover a given target.

Soft Target

The *soft target* is one who, based on his status and background, is not expected to suspect surveillance coverage. This assumes that the target has had no training in surveillance countermeasures and is not expected to employ them as a standard practice. A soft target will currently not be involved in any illegal or clandestine activity and therefore will have no reason to suspect surveillance coverage.

Hard Target

The *hard target* is one who, based on his status and background, can be expected to be surveillance conscious. A hard target represents a more sophisticated challenge to a surveillance team because he is expected to have had formal surveillance countermeasures training and might employ them during his travels as a standard practice. Common examples of hard targets are espionage agents and terrorist operatives, all of whom are thoroughly trained in surveillance-detection tactics and employ them constantly as a guarantee of survival. In most cases, such a target's training will consist of tactics that can be employed in a natural manner without displaying obvious indicators of surveillance countermeasures.

This is important to the sophisticated target because if surveillance is present and the target is observed employing surveillance countermeasures tactics, then the surveillance team will be assured that the target is in fact dirty and will intensify its efforts against him. Regardless of expected training, any target who is engaged in illegal or clandestine activity should be considered hard.

Overt Target

The *overt target* is one who, based solely on his present status, is expected to be surveillance conscious and employ surveillance countermeasures as a standard practice. The overt target represents the greatest challenge to the surveillance team because he can be expected to be more aggressive or overt in his actions. The most common example of overt targets are espionage agents operating under official diplomatic status out of official missions or embassies. Such targets constantly assume that surveillance coverage is present and will undergo a thorough ritual of surveillance detection and antisurveillance maneuvers prior to conducting any type of operational activity. Another example of an overt target is a suspected flight risk out of jail on bond.

COVER AND COVER FOR ACTION

Cover is a broad term that generally applies to any physical structure or aspect that a surveillance operator or vehicle may use to obstruct the target's view or to appear natural, when observation from the target, countersurveillance, or any third persons is possible. Physical structures such as buildings can be used as cover to conceal an operator from the target.

During a foot-surveillance operation, cover consists primarily of pedestrians in the area with which the surveillance operator can blend to appear natural. During a vehicular-surveillance operation, cover consists primarily of vehicular traffic on the roads. In both situations, the surrounding traffic enables the surveillance operator or vehicle to blend in for cover and appear as an ordinary pedestrian or vehicle. Although not a physical aspect, darkness is another form of cover that the surveillance team can use as concealment from the target.

Cover for action is a more specific term that refers to actions taken by the surveillance operator to establish a plausible reason for being in a given location or for undertaking a given activity. For example, a surveillance operator can use a telephone booth for cover, but he must actually place money in the phone and make a call to establish a cover for action. More specific applications of cover and cover for action will be addressed throughout this book.

THE SURVEILLANCE OPERATOR

Surveillance operators do not conform to any specific type in regard to physical characteristics such as gender, race, or size. In fact, it is ideal for a surveillance team to have access to as varied a mix of operators as possible to satisfy the requirements of any operation. There are, however, certain qualities that each operator should possess or aspire to develop. Some of these qualities are essential, while others can be worked around provided both that the operator realizes his weakness and the other contributions he makes to the team effort overshadow the weakness.

The first essential quality of a surveillance operator is that he must want to be a surveillance operator. The operator must thrive from the thrill of the hunt—within the obvious limitations. A disgruntled or lethargic operator will certainly lead to the failure of any surveillance operation.

Expertise in surveillance operations is obviously an important quality. The only way to establish proficiency in the art of physical surveillance is through a comprehensive knowledge of tactics and the practical application of these skills.

Inconspicuous appearance is another important quality because a surveillance team's mission is to develop information on a target without coming to his attention. The operator must not have any physical characteristics or mannerisms that make him stand out from other individuals. Scars, tattoos, or birthmarks that cannot be covered cause an operator to stand out and make it easier for a target to recognize that operator when seen a second time. Other physical characteristics such as uncorrectable limps or permanent disfigurements are detrimental for the same reasons.

The ideal operator is one who is very plain or common in appearance—the kind of person no one ever notices. Particularly tall, bulky, or overweight operators have difficulty remaining unnoticed. Particularly attractive male or female operators share this same disadvantage.

Individual judgment is an essential quality for a surveillance operator. This is the ability to use timely reason and logic in reacting to a given set of circumstances. In addition to tactical proficiency, each operator must be capable of making timely and intelligent decisions. The nature of surveillance operations do not allow for one or two highly competent operators to orchestrate the actions of all other team members. At any given time, the success or security of an entire operation may depend on the judgment of a single operator. For this reason, it is critical that each operator on the team display sound common sense and operational judgment.

Operational resourcefulness is a quality that relates directly to operator judgment. This is the ability of an operator to assess a situation quickly and maximize the possible advantages available. Resourcefulness is applied when blending with the surrounding area and adapting to unforeseen situations without drawing the target's attention. This is also the ability to think ahead of the situation and devise solutions to possible contingencies.

The surveillance operator must possess a keen sense of perception. The professional surveillance operator observes and deduces items that the common man does not. The operator must be able to read into the detail of a situation and systematically evaluate the circumstances instantly. This sense must be perpetuated in the retention of those perceptions. The surveillance operator must be able to recall events, numbers, conversations, and physical descriptions as a requisite of the profession. The ability to read lips is a valuable dimension of perception.

Physical stamina is another of the essential qualities of a surveillance operator. Surveillance operators perform challenging missions that require long hours of concentration under a high degree of stress. Because of the uniquely hazardous environment in which operators perform, they must always be of sound body and mind. Physical fatigue will invariably lead to mental errors. Such errors can compromise the operation or threaten operator safety. The surveillance operator must possess a high degree of self-restraint and patience. Much of a surveillance operation is spent sitting and waiting for something to happen. The operator must possess the mental discipline to remain focused on the mission and not become discouraged or indifferent. This only results in missed opportunities and poor security practices.

Technical proficiency is the ability to use and repair technical surveillance equipment. A surveillance team will consist of operators with varying degrees of technical proficiency, but each operator must possess basic skills in technical applications. Ideally, a team will have at least one member with the proficiency to repair communications and other technical equipment. Proficiency with photographic equipment is a critical skill for every operator. The ability to manipulate locks, penetrate computer systems, and bypass security systems are specialized skills that can support certain aspects of surveillance.

THE SURVEILLANCE CHIEF

As with any effective tactical operation, there must be one individual ultimately in charge. This individual, the *surveillance chief*, is a team member who performs tactical functions like any other operator.

The surveillance chief is not selected based on seniority or popularity; rather, he must possess the highest degree of technical and tactical proficiency. He must also possess all the qualities of a surveillance operator previously discussed. Judgment and resourcefulness are the most important of these qualities for him to possess. He must be able to display sound judgment when critical decisions regarding the overall operation are necessary. He must also be capable of employing team resources in a manner that maximizes the economy of effort.

The surveillance chief is primarily responsible for managing the preparation for a surveillance operation. He will also be the interface between the team and any other investigative or law enforcement agencies associated with the operation. During the course of a surveillance operation, the surveillance chief does little in the way of directing the activities of other team members. An effective surveillance team must rely on each of its members to possess operational proficiency and display sound tactical judgment. No one individual can, or should be expected to, make all of the decisions. Each operator must be capable of operating independently without guidance or direction. During an actual operation, the surveillance chief should rarely have to take any action above those of the other team members.

DRESS, DISGUISE, AND MANNERISMS

One of the most important qualities of a surveillance operator is the ability to blend in with his surroundings. This ensures that the operator does not stand out to the target and raise suspicion. If a target identifies the same operator in two separate locations that are not on a logical route, the operation may well be compromised. Surveillance is one of the few activities in which looks and beauty can be a disadvantage. The more unusual an operator appears in relation to the surrounding populace, the greater the possibility of subsequent recognition. For these reasons, it is essential that the operator be able to dress and act to blend in with the surrounding area and populace.

The ability to effect a change of appearance, or disguise, is also a requisite skill for any surveillance operator. Such a capability allows the operator to adapt to certain situations or to project a false identity after being exposed. (Chapter 4 discusses surveillance operation preparation in more detail.) During this stage of the operation, the operational area is researched to determine how the team can best blend with the surrounding populace. This includes an assessment of how surveillance operators should dress and conduct themselves to appear as indigenous members of the area. In operational areas where a strong ethnic representation exists, the team will be required to find an ethnic match or accept the risks. For example, if the team is to operate in a predominantly Hispanic area, it will ideally field a team of Hispanic operators. If this is impossible, the team must determine the most appropriate manner to dress and conduct itself in order to best blend with the operational area—given the identified deficiency.

Mannerisms are those characteristics or idiosyncrasies that are unique to a given operator. They are peculiarities in action or bearing. Such peculiarities include posture, stride, pace of motion, and voice quality, but the number of examples is unlimited. Mannerisms can be altered to make an operator appear more natural in a given situation. If the operator fails to concentrate on mannerisms that may stand out or appear awkward, the target's attention may be captured by these peculiarities.

Some of the most difficult mannerisms for the operator to control are those associated with nervousness and anticipation. Just as the target may become animated when conducting illegal or operational activity, the surveillance operator may become driven by the adrenaline of a surveillance operation. This can result in conspicuous actions or mannerisms such as pacing, focused staring, and continually checking a watch. The operator may also have a tendency to move more quickly or deliberately than appears natural. The only way to overcome such telling mannerisms is through operator concentration.

Other mannerisms that are unique to surveillance operators and that may draw the target's attention are those associated with the wearing of body communications equipment. Examples of these idiosyncrasies include adjusting upper-body equipment, talking into the chest, fidgeting of hands in pocket, and rubbing the ears wih fingers. The causes of such tendencies will become clear after the discussion of body communications equipment in the next chapter. Once again, these mannerisms are overcome by concentration and confidence in the use of body communications equipment.

Normally, the surveillance team will have general knowledge regarding the target's expected activities. Despite this, it is impossible for an individual operator to dress for every possible contingency. For this reason, the team must coordinate dress in advance to ensure that it begins each day, or portion of the operation, with an adequate mix of dress to integrate into as many situations as possible. This may require that different operators dress to support different contingencies. This rule of team mix will be tempered by the fact that the entire team must still be able to blend into the general operational area.

To achieve this tempered effect, the team should avoid extremes in dress unless specific information warrants it. Operators should avoid dressing to fit the most fashionable or the most casual ends of the spectrum associated with the anticipated operational area. Operators who dress close to either of the extremes will lack the flexibility to blend with the majority of the populace among that area's dress and fashion range.

Surveillance operators must take care in determining the specific types of clothing to be worn. A target who is trained and actively practices surveillance detection will accept the fact that he cannot remember all details regarding the individuals around him. For this reason, the trained target will concentrate on observing unique qualities in the appearance of surrounding individuals, which will assist in subsequent recognition at a different location. To counter this, the surveillance operator must dress in a manner that minimizes those unique aspects on which the target may key to facilitate subsequent recognition.

Operators must avoid bright or contrasting colors that stand out and are readily identifiable. Clothing should not have picture prints, designer logos, or any other wording such as university initials. Trendy or particularly stylish fashions should be avoided. In today's society, female operators are more apt to draw additional attention, particularly from a male target. For this reason tight-fitting clothing should not be worn. Hats generally stand out and should be avoided unless used for special situations.

When the weather and environment permit, it is best to layer clothing. An example of this is to wear an overcoat over a jacket with a sweater and a shirt underneath. Such a dress arrangement allows for a quick and easy change of clothing appearance by removing a layer. The operator will have less flexibility in layering in warmer weather. The concept of layering relates to the principle that it is normally easier to dress down than to dress up.

This means that generally, it is easier and quicker for an operator to go from a formal appearance to a more casual appearance. This principle dictates that the operator should begin each day or phase of the operation prepared to dress down—within the framework of a good team mix.

In selecting the appropriate clothing for surveillance operations, the first requirement is that it must be comfortable. An operator who is not comfortable in his clothing will probably not appear natural. Basic designs and bland colors are best suited for surveillance clothing. At night, dark or bland colors are particularly appropriate because brighter colors will stand out. In warmer weather, however, seasonal fashions will normally consist of brighter colors. The surveillance operator must consider this to ensure that bland clothing is not counterproductive given the dress of the surrounding populace. Shoes should be comfortable and match the operator's other attire. They should be soft-soled to avoid unnecessary or distinctive noise when near the target.

Jewelry should not be worn while on surveillance operations. In addition to the possibility of it being lost, the purpose of jewelry is to attract attention—the purpose of a surveillance operator's attire is to avoid attention. A conservative watch is natural and appropriate. Certain situations, such as following the target to an exclusive restaurant, will relax the restriction on jewelry. At night, jewelry can reflect light, thus attracting attention.

Rings and wedding sets should not be worn by surveillance operators. This should be a constant practice since wearing rings while not on operations will leave tan lines or other identifying marks. Particularly on women, hands draw immediate attention because they are an instant indicator of marital status. A naked hand with ring marks appears suspicious for a number of reasons. When the wear of jewelry is necessary, the operator must be aware of local customs and ensure that it matches the social class of the operational area. An example of adhering to local customs is that in the United States the wearing of wedding bands on the left hand is correct, but in some areas, such as some European countries, they are worn on the right hand. This consideration also applies to watches.

The style of glasses worn by an operator should look natural and blend in because they can be a very identifiable aspect of an operator's dress. Operators who are required to wear glasses for corrected vision should also own and be comfortable with contact lenses. Contacts break the general profile of glasses and can also be used to change the color of one's eyes. Although sunglasses are effective in covering identifying facial features of a surveillance operator, they will draw attention more often than not. Sunglasses should be restricted to situations in which they are worn only to blend in or enhance driver safety.

Hairstyles should be conservative and blend with the surrounding populace. This applies equally to the grooming of facial hair. The operator's hair represents the single most effective means of altering appearance. When it is consistent with the surrounding populace, hair length should initially be as long as possible. This allows the operator to change his appearance in increments by shortening hair length as the operation progresses. This concept also applies to facial hair. Male operators beginning an operation with a beard and mustache possess the ability to project at least three different appearances as the operation progresses. This must be tempered, however, with the fact that a surveillance team consisting of all bearded personnel is not appropriate.

Altering hair color is another way that hair can be used to change the appearance of an operator. Operators should use hair dyes consisting only of standard hair colors that contain no chemical components that may damage the hair's texture. They must be high-quality products that do not run or fade when wet.

Wigs and false facial hair are essential to all operators, but bald operators are absolutely ineffective without an assortment of wigs. Wigs should be custom-made for the particular operator. False facial hair should also be custom-made to ensure that the coloring and texture is consistent with the operator's real hair. Operators should apply false facial hair with a quality adhesive compound that does not degrade when wet by sweat or other sources.

There are varying degrees of disguises. They range from a basic change of appearance as a standard security precaution to a total disguise. A total disguise is used when an operator has been close enough to the target to be considered compromised and therefore must take on a completely different appearance to continue in the operation. Total disguise is also used in situations when it is anticipated that an operator will be exposed to the target. This allows the operator to project a false appearance to the target rather than exposing one that is closer to his actual appearance, which is much more difficult to disguise after the fact.

All changes of appearance must be complete. This is not to say that hair and facial appearance must be significantly altered when conducting a standard change of appearance. Dress and mannerisms can be observed from a much greater distance than facial features. It also takes a conscious effort to recall facial features, whereas the dress and mannerisms of operators are more likely to be stored in the subconscious of the target. The operator will normally know when he has received the conscious scrutiny of the target, thus warranting a complete disguise.

In making a change of appearance complete, there should be no visible indication to the target of the change. Observing the same operator twice in different locations is suspicious; seeing the same operator in one location with a beard and then seeing him in a second location without the beard but wearing the same shirt compromises the operation. A target will be certain that he is under surveillance if he detects individuals using disguises in his presence. This is why it is important that changes of appearance are complete rather than partial. They should consist of an alteration of hair grooming and a change of all exposed items of clothing. This must include jewelry, watches, glasses, and shoes. Some of the most sophisticated espionage organizations train their operatives to key on shoes when observing surrounding individuals for surveillance detection purposes. This is done because when surveillance operators change their appearance, they are normally reluctant to discard their favorite and most comfortable pair of shoes.

In preparing for a surveillance operation, the individual operator must anticipate the requirement for change of appearance and disguise. Each operator should carry sufficient clothing to accommodate any situation. Most changes of appearance will be conducted in a surveillance vehicle while the operation is ongoing. Each operator should have a customized disguise kit with items such as hair-coloring dyes, hair-styling gel, false facial hair, and wigs.

The complete change of appearance will also include a change in mannerisms. Recall that mannerisms are easily observed and retained in both the conscious and subconscious memory. As with clothing, a target may be able to detect a disguise by noticing an operator with different clothing but the same mannerisms as those observed previously. Such alterations in mannerism are normally as simple as altering posture, stride, and pace of motion. Uncontrollable mannerisms such as limping, coughing, or wheezing will normally restrict the effectiveness of an operator in a continued operation.

3

SURVEILLANCE
EQUIPMENT
OVERVIEW

The professional surveillance team consists of intelligent operators with a high degree of tactical and technical proficiency. The operator who masters the surveillance skills explained in this book will possess the tactical expertise to operate at any level. This book, however, is not intended to provide detail regarding all the technical equipment applications necessary to complement a tactically sound effort. This would require a book in itself and detract from the focus of physical surveillance.

Technical proficiency with surveillance equipment is an integral aspect of the art of surveillance. This chapter will expose the reader to the types of equipment that are employed to enhance the effectiveness of a surveillance effort.

When the surveillance team or operator identifies the equipment that best suits needs and budget, specialized training and practice should be tailored for that specific type of equipment. Initially, the training should begin with the information provided in the user's manual that accompanies the particular item of equipment. Practical applications in the use of the equipment develops proficiency. If additional expertise is required, then practical training from a technical expert should be commissioned.

It is important that a surveillance team maintain perspective when determining the equipment that is appropriate for its particular needs. Some types of equipment are basic necessities required for physical surveillance operations. Other types of equipment improve the baseline capability, but the marginal returns may be negligible. This is primarily the case with sophisticated equipment that is many times too expensive, sensitive, and complicated for extensive use. A surveillance team with the resources to acquire state-of-the-art equipment must not lose sight of the element that makes it function—the human element. Regardless of price, surveillance equipment is only as effective as the operator using it.

Ninety-eight percent of an operation is effectively discharged through the use of surveillance vehicles, communications equipment, maps, cameras, and binoculars. Any other equipment is a luxury and should not be employed at the expense of forgoing the basics in equipment and training. When these basics are satisfied, the team with the resources to acquire sophisticated systems can then consider an enhanced operational effectiveness.

MAPPING

Adequate mapping of any given area of operations is essential to the success of a surveillance operation. Normally during an actual surveillance, only one surveillance operator or vehicle will have visual command of the target at any given time. This requires that the entire team have corresponding maps to identify the location of the target so the members can orient themselves as to their location in relation to the target.

The maps used for surveillance operations should be book-type maps that fit comfortably in the lap. Map books are ideal because they cover a large area in great detail. Foldout maps are inadequate because they are too large and cumbersome for secure and effective operations. Foldout maps also do not cover enough area in sufficient detail for most operations. The ability for a surveillance operator to read a map while riding in a vehicle and still look natural when in sight of the target is yet another factor making map books more effective than foldouts.

Map detail is of paramount importance in selecting the appropriate map book for an operation. Mapping must be current and accurate. This is a critical consideration since most of the team will orient themselves on the map at any given time during the operation. The surveillance operator with visual command of the target must be able to transmit accurate target locations in order for the entire team to have a timely and accurate fix on the target. When possible, the mapping should include details regarding public transportation systems, such as mass transit and bus routes. If this is not possible, the team must acquire supplemental maps of the public transportation systems. In addition to detailed mapping of the city in which the operation is anticipated, broad-coverage maps such as atlases should be acquired for each surveillance vehicle.

Given adequate time to prepare, maps can be modified to enhance the efficiency of an operation. One such method of preparing a map is referred to as *dotting*. As the term implies, dotting consists of sticking adhesive dots to the maps at prominent road intersections, terrain features, and landmarks. The dots are numbered identically in all corresponding map books. This practice enables the surveillance operator or surveillance vehicle with visual command of the target to transmit the target's location and direction of travel to the entire team by identifying the appropriate numbered dot. By using such a dot system, an operator does not have to waste valuable time on the radio network by naming streets or landmarks. Different-colored dots can be used to add another dimension of detail to the dotting system. The color of the dot selected should correspond as closely as possible to the colors on the map. For example, if city streets are the color red, then the dots corresponding to city street options should also be red.

SURVEILLANCE VEHICLES

Proper surveillance vehicles are essential equipment for any surveillance operation. Surveillance vehicles represent the most prominent and highly visible aspect of a surveillance team. Even during a foot surveillance, vehicles may be used in support.

Surveillance Vehicle Specifications

There are basic qualities in surveillance vehicles that should be maintained in order to ensure an effective and secure operation.

Maintenance

Surveillance vehicles must be well maintained. The very nature of a surveillance operation imposes a high degree of stress on a vehicle. Surveillance vehicles must be mechanically sound to ensure that a failure in vehicle performance does not compromise the success, security, or safety of an operation. Noisy brake pads are but one of many mechanical deficiencies that may make a surveillance vehicle stand out to the target. All surveillance vehicle lights must be in proper working order. Nonfunctional lights present a signature that the target may identify and recognize again in the future. Dents and large scratches are also unacceptable because they too present a significant signature that may be recognized, thus jeopardizing the operation.

Speed

Speed is an essential criterion for surveillance vehicles. They must be capable of fast acceleration from both static and moving positions. They must also be capable of running at high rates of speed for extended periods.

Make and Model

Surveillance vehicle make and model should be consistent with the other vehicles indigenous to the area in which the operation will be conducted. This will ensure that the surveillance vehicles blend with the surrounding traffic.

Tags and Stickers

Care should also be taken to ensure that the surveillance vehicles have license plates and inspection stickers that are consistent with those of other vehicles in the area. As with the clothing of individual operators, the color of surveillance vehicles must be inconspicuous. Bright colors and identifying paint designs should be avoided. Colors such as tan, gray, dark blue, and nonmetallic silver are normally best.

Size

Surveillance vehicle size should be adequate to support a sophisticated surveillance effort. They should be medium- to large-sized, four-door sedans. Since much of the time during a surveillance operation is spent in surveillance vehicles, they should be as comfortable as possible. The vehicles should have four doors, due to the number of operators who may be expected to enter and exit quickly. The trunk should be large enough to accommodate the significant equipment and clothing requirements of a surveillance operation. In addition to these requirements for a large trunk, covert photographic equipment is commonly fitted into the rear lights or the trunk keyhole and must be operated by an individual in the trunk of the vehicle.

Fuel Economy

In light of the requirement for size, surveillance vehicles should provide adequate fuel economy for uninterrupted operational use. Large fuel tank capacity should also be a selection criterion.

Automatic Transmissions

Vehicles with automatic transmissions are generally best suited for surveillance operations. In some circumstances the driver of a surveillance vehicle may be required to operate alone. This requires that the driver operate the surveillance vehicle, observe the target, operate the communications equipment, read a map, and take notes at the same time. An automatic transmission is one less distractor to occupy the driver's free hand as opposed to a manual transmission. Manual-transmission vehicles do provide an advantage in that they generally accelerate faster than automatics, particularly while moving. Manual-transmission vehicles can also be slowed by downshifting rather than engaging the brake, which can be an advantage when travelling in front of the target.

Surveillance Vehicle Modifications

After the appropriate surveillance vehicles have been selected for a surveillance operation, a number of specialized modifications can be made to enhance their effectiveness. The primary purpose of surveillance vehicle modifications is either to enhance their technical capability for operational effectiveness or to diversify their signature for operational security.

Signature

The term *signature* refers to any qualities of a surveillance vehicle by which it can be identified. The ability to change any of these qualities, or the signature, of a surveillance vehicle during the course of an operation is essential to security. A surveillance vehicle's signature will consist of any number of characteristics that may stand out and allow it to be identified more than once by the target, thus raising suspicions. The number of possible signature changes that a surveillance vehicle can undergo during the course of an operation will be determined by the amount of exposure to the target and limited only by the operator's imagination. The only precaution is that the signature change should not be so extreme that it makes the surveillance vehicle stand out from other surrounding vehicles.

A number of miscellaneous modifications can be made to change the signature of a surveillance vehicle. Signature changes can be as simple as washing the vehicle, attaching magnetic decals, adding child-restraining seats, or attaching a ski rack, as appropriate. Rental or dealership stickers represent a unique signature and should be removed. In some circumstances, it may be more expedient to change the signature by repainting a surveillance vehicle that has been compromised rather than taking the time to install equipment in another vehicle.

A significant aspect of a surveillance vehicle's signature is its license plate. This identifies a vehicle by state or area and more specifically by number to the keen observer. A surveillance vehicle will have a lower signature if its license plate has a nondescript number and blends in with other surrounding vehicles. Particularly in nonmetropolitan U.S. areas, out-of-state license plates draw immediate attention. This signature problem is compounded in European countries, where each vehicle is identified by beginning letters that are unique to its city of origin.

The surveillance team should take the appropriate precautions to prevent the target from tracing the license plates to the team or one of its operators. When renting vehicles, the operators may choose to falsify their identities on rental documents.

The falsification of rental documents may, however, result in legal considerations that the team is unwilling to accept. Another option is to purchase or rent surveillance vehicles under the name of a cover agency or company that cannot be associated directly with the team or its operators. Payment for vehicles should always be made in cash or another form that cannot be traced to the team. As the license plate of a surveillance vehicle is compromised or the team moves into a state or area in which the indigenous vehicles bear different plates, the security of the operation is degraded.

When time does not allow for new surveillance vehicles to be locally acquired and equipped, it is favorable to have the flexibility to change the license plates of existing surveillance vehicles. Such a capability normally takes extensive preparation and coordination. Without official coordination the team must either alter registration documents or bear plates with no corresponding documentation. In either case, legal considerations will represent a significant risk to the overall operation. If appropriate, quick-change license plate brackets can be installed, which will allow the operators to change license plates and continue with the mission in a matter of seconds. Unless required by law, the front of a surveillance vehicle should not bear any type of identifying plate.

Communications Equipment

The most basic yet most important modification to a surveillance vehicle is a radio communications system. This modification will be discussed thoroughly in the communications equipment section of this chapter, but its importance warrants particular emphasis. The installation of communications equipment in each surveillance vehicle is essential to a coordinated team effort. Surveillance operations employing more than one surveillance vehicle cannot be conducted effectively without radio communications. Hand-held radios are not adequate for surveillance operations because they lack sufficient power to transmit over the distance and terrain required of most operations. Additionally, hand-held radios must be placed closer to the mouth in order to transmit. This represents an unacceptable risk that the radio may be seen by the target or third persons who may pose a risk to the security of the operation.

Lights

Surveillance vehicle light modifications are made to both enhance security and alter surveillance vehicle signature. These modifications primarily affect night operations. The most common such modification is to manipulate headlights so that their brightness and level can be manually adjusted by the driver. Through such adjustments, the same surveillance vehicle can project a different signature to the target from one portion of the follow to another, thus projecting the illusion of being a different vehicle. The archaic tactic of modifying vehicle lights so that one of the headlights can be killed completely is not viable in professional operations. An important principle of signature changes is that they be significant enough to make the surveillance vehicle appear different, but not so pronounced that they draw undue interest from the target. Any vehicle on the road with only one functional headlight will gain such interest. Any additional scrutiny from the target may permit him to identify other unique qualities that may make future detection easier.

Another surveillance vehicle light modification is the installation of brake-light and reverse-light kill switches. By splicing a circuit breaker directly into the power wires of the brake lights and reverse lights respectively, two kill switches can be connected and installed under the driver's control panel. The brake-light kill option is used primarily when the surveillance vehicle is in front of the target vehicle. By engaging the brake-light kill switch, the surveillance vehicle can slow to maintain pace with the target vehicle without displaying that it is braking and slowing unnaturally. This kill switch should be installed in such a manner that it must be depressed the entire time that the system is in use. This ensures that the system is not inadvertently left on, causing a safety and security risk.

The reverse-light kill switch should be installed in such a manner that it can be engaged to remain on and disengaged at will. This kill option is generally used in conjunction with the brake-light kill option in circumstances when the target is stopped and it is too dark to see the surveillance vehicle unless its lights are on. In such circumstances both kill switches can be engaged, with the vehicle lights off, to allow the surveillance vehicle to maneuver without being detected by the target.

MOBILE-SURVEILLANCE SYSTEMS

Mobile surveillance systems are specialized vehicles that have been specially equipped to perform technical surveillance functions beyond the capability of a standard surveillance vehicle. Most mobile surveillance systems are installed in vans because of the amount of equipment involved with such a system. Despite the significant equipment modifications, the vehicle will appear natural to any outside observation. The van is completely enclosed so that the equipment inside and any operators manning that equipment are concealed from outside observation.

These specialized vehicles will perform a number of functions that a standard surveillance vehicle or individual operator cannot. They may be employed as an observation post to discreetly observe the actions of a target in a location where a standard surveillance vehicle with operators would risk detection. They can serve as a control base for a portion of the surveillance operation or perform specialized photography or videotaping missions. They may also serve as listening posts for technical monitoring devices or telephone taps.

A surveillance team will rarely possess the expertise to develop its own mobile-surveillance system with all the capabilities organic to a totally integrated system. Many of the equipment specifications involved require the expertise of manufacturing agencies that specialize in the development of such equipment. Since a total mobile-surveillance capability can run $75,000 or more, it is beyond the financial means of most surveillance teams. Yet with some technical capability and knowledge of mobile surveillance systems, any team can equip a moderately priced van with capabilities tailored to specific requirements. A fully equipped mobile-surveillance system consists of the following:

- A specially configured and concealed electrical system with additional power sources
- Soundproof insulated panels to prevent the activities conducted inside the vehicle from being audible on the outside
- Stabilization pegs that are inserted into the axle when the vehicle is parked, which prevent the surveillance vehicle from shaking as operators move around inside

- A covert periscope with a 360-degree field of view for photography, videotaping, and observation post capability; additional camera equipment may be mounted to complement this capability
- A receiver, recorder, and earphones for listening post technical monitoring missions
- An integrated communications system with additional power amplification for control base capability
- A cellular telephone with an adjustable volume control and incoming-call indication lights for silent operation
- A climate control system
- Toilet facilities and a refrigerator

COMMUNICATIONS EQUIPMENT

The most important aspect of a comprehensive surveillance team effort is an integrated communications system. The system must network all surveillance vehicles and foot operators on a common frequency. Such a system allows the entire team to maneuver in support of the operation based on the observations of only one operator or vehicle.

For example, with a combined vehicular and foot surveillance (Chapter 10) consisting of six surveillance vehicles and 12 operators, the operation may progress to the point of six foot operators on the ground with six surveillance vehicles in support. This scenario would allow for only one of those foot operators with command of the target to transmit pertinent information to the entire team. This capability allows 11 other team assets to maneuver in support of the operation over an area ranging for many miles with only one operator actually observing the target.

Encryption Systems

Surveillance team communications are always vulnerable to interception. A sophisticated surveillance target may use a radio scanner for surveillance detection purposes. At any given time, there may be a number of law enforcement agencies or amateur enthusiasts scanning the airwaves for significant activity. For these reasons, it is ideal to have a communications system that can be secured by encryption. This restricts anyone monitoring the surveillance team's frequency from hearing the details of the operation. The only indication of activity on the frequency will be a rush of static when a radio is transmitting.

Encrypted systems can be broken by recording the signal and replaying it through a computerized deciphering program. This method does not yield real-time information and is only practiced by the most sophisticated intelligence agencies. Whether or not the system is encrypted, the surveillance team should use brevity codes to deter any intercepting element from identifying the target or the specific location of the operation. (Appendix A contains an example of brevity codes for use in surveillance operations. Appendix B is an explanation of brevity code use.) Another way to minimize the possibility of interception is to employ frequencies that are not commonly used in the area. Radios with a frequency-hopping capability further enhance security. This capability consists of radios that change transmission frequencies at nonstandard intervals, making them extremely difficult to monitor constantly.

Body Communications Equipment

The capability to equip each of the team's operators with a body communications system is one of the factors that sets a truly professional surveillance team apart from the others in the business. The ability for each operator to communicate simultaneously with all of the team's operators and surveillance vehicles raises the team's effectiveness to a significant level.

Body communications equipment must be small enough to be concealed naturally under the clothing of the operator. There are a number of equipment packages on the market that will satisfy the requirements of any team. The complex aspects of the communications equipment necessitates that the team acquire a prepared package rather than attempting to develop its own systems. There are a number of peculiarities in the system, such as cutting the antenna to the correct length to match the radio's frequency. Unless the team has dedicated technical support or an operator who is a radio technician, the difficulties in developing a system will be overwhelming. When purchasing a communications system the team should also establish a service contract.

A covert system consists of a radio, a three-wire adaptor set, a wire antenna, and an earpiece. Radios that have been designed for body use come with an adaptor to attach the three-wire set. The three-wire adaptor set consists of a microphone, an inductor, and a transmitter button. These three items are attached into a common plug at the end, with sufficient wire to meet the specifications of the operator.

The earpieces should be formfitting to position securely and naturally in the ear. When properly in place, the earpiece should be undetectable unless given particular scrutiny. The radio should be worn in a custom-made harness. Most operators will wear the radio on their upper bodies, but some may select to wear it on their thighs or ankles under baggy pants or a dress. The radio must be held firmly to the body and not protrude visibly through the clothing. Harnesses configured similarly to pistol harnesses are normally appropriate. Perhaps the best type of radio harness is a large elastic band that is either pulled over or Velcro-fastened around the upper body. With a shoulder strap sewn on and a pocket sewn in for the radio, this type of harness will hold the radio firmly to the upper body with relatively little protrusion.

The three-wire adaptor set is plugged into the radio and also concealed completely under the clothing. The wired microphone will be pinned to the radio harness in a location that is generally in the center of the chest. Female operators can pin the microphone to their brassieres. The microphones are sensitive enough to easily pick up the operator's speech from this location.

The wired inductor will be attached to the harness, or taped, over the collarbone on the opposite side of the body from which the radio is positioned. If the radio is not worn on the upper body, this precaution is not necessary. The earpiece is worn in the ear that is on the same side of the body as the inductor. The inductor will transmit incoming radio transmissions to the earpiece. This precludes the need for a wire running up the neck to the earpiece, as is common to most Secret Service agents surrounding the president. Unlike Secret Service agents who want to make their presence known, the surveillance operator's equipment must be completely undetectable.

The wired transmitter button will be placed in a position that allows the operator to engage easily and discreetly for transmissions. The transmitter button is most commonly wired down under the pants and into the front pocket through a small hole cut in its inner lining. Such placement allows the operator to transmit by casually placing his hand in the pocket.

The wire antenna is screwed into the same location on the radio as the standard antenna. This antenna is an extremely flexible wire insulated with plastic. The antenna is very small in diameter and has qualities of flexibility that are similar to those of a piece of string. The antenna is cut to a length that matches the frequency of the radio system. The antenna is draped back over the shoulder opposite to the side on which the inductor is positioned, and secured down the center of the back by the harness or tape.

The radio and earpiece are both battery powered. The earpiece uses a small battery with a normal life of at least 24 hours. Operators should always carry extra earpiece batteries for continued operation. The life of radio batteries is determined by their size. The trade-off in this case is that the longer the battery life, the larger the radio unit and the more difficult it is to conceal. The operator must select a battery size that is appropriate for the operation. When possible, an extra battery should be carried to ensure continued operation. Female operators can carry additional batteries in their purses, but male operators must be more resourceful.

Surveillance Vehicle Communications Equipment

The proper system for surveillance vehicle communications consists of a hand-held radio, communications converter with a wire-remote microphone, power amplifier, speaker, and vehicle-mounted antenna. Such equipment is manufactured as an integrated system and is available from a number of companies specializing in communications equipment.

The system is operated by placing a hand-held radio in the communications converter. The communications converter consists of a wire-remoted hand-held microphone and the volume and squelch controls. The communications converter allows the radio to be operated by the hand-held microphone and transmits incoming radio traffic over a wire-connected speaker. The converter also feeds power to the inserted radio unit, thus negating concern over the limited battery life. The power amplifier is a wired interface between the communications converter and the vehicle-mounted antenna. The power amplifier serves to increase the transmission power of the system by up to 10 times that of the hand-held unit when used alone. This results in a significant increase in transmission range.

The surveillance vehicle communications system should be installed in a manner that conceals all the equipment from the casual observer. Obviously, if the target or even third persons observe communications equipment in a surveillance vehicle, the operation is significantly compromised. The best location to install the communications converter is either under the passenger seat or in the glove compartment. Since the communications system will normally be controlled by an operator in the passenger seat, these locations make use easier. The exception to this placement is when the system will be operated solely by the driver. In such cases the communications converter should be installed under the driver's seat. The system's speaker should be installed under the seat opposite the seat under which the converter is installed, or under one of the back seats. The speaker should not be collocated with the converter because the converter may cause feedback between the speaker and the microphone.

The power amplifier should be installed in the trunk of the surveillance vehicle since it requires no manual manipulation during the course of an operation. The system antenna should be mounted covertly in the place of the surveillance vehicle's radio antenna to appear as such. More than one antenna is indicative of some type of communications system and may be identified by the target.

The entire surveillance vehicle communications system will be powered by the vehicle battery. The system should be wired in a manner that allows it to be powered without the ignition power engaged. This requires that an independent power switch be installed to operate the communications system when the surveillance vehicle is not running. The microphone is operated by wire remote from the communications converter in a manner that allows easy use by an operator in the passenger or driver's seat. It is essential that the microphone be sensitive enough to pick up the operator's speech while being held down in the lap or next to either thigh. A professional surveillance operator does not place the microphone to the mouth as Hollywood would lead to believe. This places the microphone in view of surrounding traffic and perhaps even the target—an unacceptable and unnecessary security risk.

An equipment modification that alleviates the use of a handheld microphone altogether is a hands-free system. A small microphone can be placed out of sight above the visor or within the interior roof insulation liner. A push-to-talk control is installed in the front right floorboard of the passenger side and in the front left floorboard of the driver side. This enables the operator to transmit traffic by keying the microphone by foot, thus freeing the hands for other operational tasks.

One security consideration that accompanies any vehicle communications system is the risk of radio traffic being heard from outside the vehicle by surrounding traffic or even the target. When surveillance operators are wearing body communications with earpieces, this risk can be negated. A coil induction system can be installed within the interior roof insulation liner. This consists of a loop coil inductor that is wired to the communications converter. Any incoming radio traffic is transmitted from the coil inductor directly to the body communications equipment of the operators in the vehicles, thus making no external noise.

When such a specialized system is not used, body communications equipment must be turned off when inside the surveillance vehicle. In addition to unnecessary battery drain, active body communications equipment will produce feedback with the surveillance vehicle system. It is particularly important for operators to remember to turn their equipment off before entering the surveillance vehicle. If this is not done, feedback will be transmitted over the radio network to all surveillance vehicles and operators. This may interfere with ongoing transmissions or cause a security risk for other surveillance vehicles.

Specially configured portable communications equipment kits can be developed for contingency installation in surveillance vehicles. This consists of the communications converter, speaker, and power amplifier configured in an easily transportable case such as a suitcase. Such a system can be easily installed in a vehicle that is not equipped with communications equipment. The system should have a plug adaptor that will fit into the cigarette lighter for a power source if time does not permit wiring to the vehicle battery.

This type of system is not ideal, but it is effective in making a new surveillance vehicle immediately mission ready. This should be used only as an interim solution until the vehicle can be properly equipped. One primary drawback is that unless some time can be taken to mount a covert antenna, the system must operate with a magnetically mounted antenna, which is less than discreet. Additionally, the equipment is more readily detectable through outside observation.

The installation of a cellular telephone unit in each of the team's surveillance vehicles will significantly enhance the effectiveness of the overall communications capability. Vehicle phones can be used to discuss operational matters that are too detailed to tie up the radio network over. A phone also provides the team with a communications link to individuals/agencies not actively engaged in the surveillance operation. Surveillance vehicles that are out of radio range with the rest of the team or have radio communications failure can contact the team via phone. Additionally, foot operators who have lost radio contact for whatever reason can contact the team from a pay phone. As the reader progresses through this book, the importance of surveillance vehicle telephones will become apparent. A surveillance team should also maintain portable telephone units for a number of possible applications.

PHOTOGRAPHIC, VIDEO, AND OBSERVATION EQUIPMENT

Photographs and video are the most effective methods of confirming the observations of the surveillance effort to a skeptical client or jury. Expertise in the use of a camera for surveillance photography is a critical skill for any professional operator. The operator must be knowledgeable in aspects of light, speed, and film selection for any given situation. A comprehensive discussion of all aspects regarding surveillance photography warrants a book in itself. A surveillance team must place photography training among its highest priorities and commission professional guidance if such expertise is needed.

Photography

Camera

The 35mm camera is the standard for surveillance purposes. The 35mm is adaptable to other surveillance accessories and hosts all of the film formats necessary for any situation encountered by the surveillance operator. The model selected should be durable yet reliable. It should be equipped with a built-in light meter to assist the operator in adjusting the camera to the appropriate f-number and aperture setting. Automatic focusing is essential for both the novice and seasoned surveillance operator. The camera selected should have a bayonet-type lens mount for fast and easy lens changes. A motor-drive connection and a remote release capability are also desirable specifications. Miniature and subminiature cameras are valuable in circumstances requiring extreme discretion.

Lenses

A complete set of camera lenses will include the 28mm, 35mm, 50mm, 100mm, 135mm, 300mm, and 600mm. Telephoto and zoom lenses further enhance the camera's capability. A 50mm lens is adequate for most standard surveillance practices, but a 300mm is the lens of choice when optimum identification quality under discreet conditions is required. The lenses selected should be fast enough to facilitate effective low-light photography.

Film

Film selection is another critical aspect of photography effectiveness. (The use of infrared film for night photography will be addressed in Chapter 13.) Infrared film facilitates a number of surveillance applications in addition to night photography. These include thermal imaging; detection of secret writing or falsified/altered documents; the examination of the contents of a sealed envelope; and photography through smoke, fog, and haze.

A capable operator with the proper camera equipment and film can attain an identification-quality photograph in nearly any condition and at a considerable distance.

Motor Drives

One common deficiency in surveillance photography is that it is difficult to record a sequence of events through still photography. Battery-powered motor drive winders can be attached to a camera for a rapid succession of photographs to record a sequence of events. The power winder, however, is not always feasible for surveillance operations because it increases the size of the camera and emits an audible clicking sound. The use of a motor drive also adds another consideration for the operator when setting the camera specifications and selecting film. A final limiting factor to the use of a power winder is that a camera only has the film capacity to photograph a sequence of events for a matter of seconds.

Videotaping

Videotaping is an excellent method of recording a sequence of events to be used as evidence or for other purposes. A primary detractor to videotape is that it may not always be possible to attain the resolution necessary for a positive identification of the target, which will be necessary in a court of law. This is the case because it is normally necessary to freeze a video frame in order to identify an individual on the video. This process normally provides a poor-quality image even when developed into a hard copy with a video graphics printer. When possible, the ideal solution is to record the target's activity with both still photographic and video coverage when it is anticipated that he will conduct illegal or operational activity. This provides identification-quality photography while capturing the circumstances relating to the photographs. In any case, 16mm taping will yield a higher-quality product for identification and presentation purposes than 8mm because of the larger film format. A date/time indicator will also lend credibility to videotape that is offered as evidence. Photography quality is normally clearer when the camera can be stabilized by a tripod or other similar means. This is particularly the case when an observation post is employed (see Chapter 5).

Remote Observation

Still photography and video cameras can be manipulated remotely, given the appropriate equipment. Just as security cameras in banks are monitored from a standoff location, a surveillance team can position cameras in concealed locations without being manned. The most basic method is to remote-wire the camera to a video monitor and recorder. When wired transmission is not appropriate, a video camera can be monitored via a microwave transmission. This is done by attaching a transmitter to the camera, which sends a signal with the video image to a receiver for monitoring and recording. The ability to remotely manipulate the position of the camera requires a mechanical platform and some basic knowledge of electronics.

The acquisition or development of covert camera packages provides a valuable capability for any surveillance effort. Covert camera packages are specialized kits that are concealed in an item, such as a briefcase or a purse, and can be used in sight of the target without drawing attention. The camera equipment will be wired in such a manner that it can be controlled by the operator who is carrying the package—for example, by placing a button on the base of a briefcase hand grip. The ability to construct and use such packages requires a high degree of expertise. An operator must practice extensively with the kit to become comfortable in positioning the package and acquiring quality pictures or videotape of the target in a natural manner. One method of overcoming the difficulty required in positioning the camera is through the use of microwave transmitters and receivers, as discussed previously. Assuming that the operator who is employing the covert package has body communications equipment, the camera can be positioned by an operator who is monitoring its image remotely. The operator monitoring the camera will direct the operator with the covert package as to how to position the package to get a focus on the target.

A surveillance team should maintain its own film-processing capability. This will require that at least one member of the team possess the requisite expertise in film development. In many situations it may be necessary to process film immediately to support the continued operation. With the appropriate chemicals and equipment, this can be done in a hotel room. Commercial film-processing establishments may not be able to accommodate the immediate needs of the surveillance team. Additionally, pictures taken in support of a surveillance operation will normally be sensitive to the supported investigation. Such photographs are distinct from those normally processed by commercial establishments, because it will be obvious to the curious developer that the photographs were taken surreptitiously. This can result in a security compromise that may be unacceptable to the surveillance team or the supported investigative agency.

Observation-enhancing equipment consists primarily of binoculars or monocular telescopes. Binoculars serve a very important purpose in any surveillance operation. Ideally, each surveillance vehicle will carry two sets of binoculars. One set will be a small hand-size model for discreet use and concealed carrying by an operator on foot. The second set will be the standard-size, long-range binoculars for maximum visibility when discretion is not a requirement. Gyro-stabilized binoculars provide a steady long-range observation capability from moving vehicles, boats, and aircraft, which is difficult to attain with standard binoculars. (Observation-enhancing equipment for use at night or in low-light situations, such as night-vision devices and flashlights, will be discussed in Chapter 13.)

One final item of discussion in regard to observation equipment is the identification kit. Although these will rarely stand as judicial evidence, they are a valuable tool for still imaging. This is an effective method of developing a composite picture of an individual of interest to the team who was observed during a surveillance operation but was not photographed. The identification kit is a comprehensive set of facial features, shapes, and hair-type designs. Separate designs can be superimposed to develop a likeness of the individual who was observed. This composite picture can be distributed to other investigative agencies for identification or used by the team as a basis for future identification. The identification kit is easily mastered but should not be entrusted to a novice for operational purposes.

TECHNICAL MONITORING EQUIPMENT

Electronic monitoring equipment serves a number of purposes in a surveillance operation. Such equipment has been critical to the success of many operations, but it can also represent the demise of a team that relies more on technical capabilities than the tactics of physical surveillance. Technical monitoring is simply a tool to enhance the effectiveness of a physical surveillance. When the objectives of an investigation can be satisfied through the use of technical monitoring equipment alone, it is termed a *monitoring mission* and not a surveillance operation. This a job for technicians and not surveillance operators. There are, however, very credible applications for technical monitoring in support of physical surveillance operations.

Technical capability is expensive and requires a high degree of expertise to employ effectively. This discussion will serve only as an introduction to technical monitoring and some of its applications to physical surveillance. It is not intended to provide the information and expertise required for such complicated activities. For the purposes of this discussion, technical monitoring devices will be categorized as 1) technical listening devices, 2) technical video devices, and 3) technical tracking devices.

Technical Listening Devices

Technical listening devices are used in support of surveillance operations to develop information that will assist the team in anticipating the actions of the target. Obviously, if the team knows in advance the time and location in which a significant activity will take place, it will be better prepared to cover such a situation. Listening devices, or bugs, are the most common of all technical listening capabilities. They can be placed in any location in which the target may be expected to discuss information of operational interest. The primary obstacle to the use of listening devices is gaining access to the area to be bugged, normally requiring surreptitious entry. An alternative to clandestine entry is to recruit a source who has access to the location or can give the team such access. Another alternative is to install the device in an item that the target intends to take into the premises or one that is sent and accepted by the target. This practice may be the riskier of the two if the target is skeptical or paranoid.

Battery Powered

A primary restricting factor to any listening device is power. Battery-powered devices must be serviced periodically to change the power source. This requires that the surveillance team gain repeated access to the premises for continued use. Some sophisticated devices possess a low-power, low-output capability or battery-saving circuitry to enhance battery life.

Electrical Implants

When possible, it is most effective to install the listening device so that it is wired to the electrical system of the premises. Listening devices planted in electrical appliances will have a power source provided that the appliance remains plugged in. An excellent location for bugs, all other factors being equal, is behind a power socket. This gives an immediate power source to the listening device with little relative interference. Ready-to-install, power-socket listening devices are available.

Wire Transmission vs. Transmitted Signals

Listening devices are monitored either by wire transmission or by transmitted signals. *Wire-transmitted devices* are more secure in the sense that they do not emit as strong a signal at the source. This makes the device much less vulnerable to detection from technical surveillance countermeasures equipment. Additionally, because the signal is transmitted via a wire it is not susceptible to detection by spectrum-scanning equipment or accidental intercept. A critical advantage to wired devices is that when not powered by a constant power source, they can be powered by direct current through the same line that is used for monitoring. This negates concern over limited battery life. Wire transmissions also provide better-quality audio resolution than wireless transmissions because they are not affected by environmental interference factors.

The limiting factor in wire transmissions is that the monitoring activity can only be a wire's length away from the source. This may not pose a problem when monitoring an adjoining hotel room, but it will be when the device is planted in a more remote location such as a house. Additionally, if the device is discovered, the wire will lead to the location of the monitoring activity. In ideal circumstances, however, wired devices can be monitored over a greater distance when the wired connection can be extended.

Wireless Devices

Wireless devices are restricted to transmission range but generally provide more flexibility in the location of the monitoring activity. The monitoring activity can be established in a listening post with a receiver that is anywhere within the range of the transmitter. Listening posts will normally be established in a residence or vehicle. Transmission range can be extended by the use of relay devices such as a repeater. The quality of gain or sensitivity in the transmissions receiver will also affect the monitoring range.

The limiting factor in wireless transmissions is that they are highly susceptible to detection by technical surveillance countermeasures equipment and signals intercept. One method to minimize this vulnerability is to use devices that transmit on nonstandard frequencies. This reduces the probability of transmitting on a frequency that is in use in the area or in a frequency range that is commonly monitored by police agencies or amateur enthusiasts. Other methods of minimizing the probability of intercept include frequency modulation, frequency hopping, frequency snuggling, noise masking, and burst-transmitted data.

Active vs. Passive Devices

Listening devices can be further categorized as either *active* or *passive*. Active listening devices have continuous power emissions and transmit constantly. Passive listening devices can be activated when required and only emit and transmit when activated. These can either be voice activated at the source or command activated by the monitoring activity. Active devices, therefore, are constantly vulnerable to technical detection whereas passive devices are only vulnerable when activated. Passive devices make more economical use of their power supply because they only draw power when activated. These factors make passive listening devices preferable to active devices.

Telephone Monitoring

Telephone monitoring is another form of technical listening that can be used to support a surveillance operation. Telephones can be manipulated to monitor conversations in the vicinity of the phone unit as well as a two-party conversation when the telephone is in use. One method of telephone monitoring is to install a listening device in the phone itself. Obviously the device will be a wireless transmitter. The primary limiting factor in the installation of such devices is that they are more susceptible to detection through a physical inspection of the telephone.

The other form of telephone monitoring is through line inter-cept, or tapping. Depending on the degree of expertise in this area, a target's telephone can be tapped anywhere between the telephone unit and the main telephone exchange servicing the initial microwave link. The farther away the tap is from the source, the greater the level of expertise and research required. Additionally, the farther away from the source, the poorer the quality of the intercept. The primary limiting factor in wiretap-ping is that a wire is normally required between the tap and the monitoring location. As with wire-transmitted listening devices, detection of the tap will lead to the location of the monitoring activity. Although a wired intercept is the most common applica-tion, there are signal-transmitting devices that can be attached to the telephone wire. Cellular or cordless phones are highly sus-ceptible to intercept by standard frequency monitors.

Technical listening can also be conducted through the use of specialized microphones that are manned at the source from an adjacent room or outside of a premises. These are high-sensitivity directional or parabolic microphones that are wired to a high-gain, low-noise amplifier. The amplifier is monitored by an oper-ator with headphones and is equipped to feed a tape recorder. Such a system can also be employed to intercept conversations in open areas. This application requires favorable conditions because of the sensitivity of the microphone, which will pick up intermediate noise, thus degrading the quality of the intercept. The monitoring location is more restricted when using direction-al microphones because a line-of-sight application is required. Additionally, sensitive headset microphone units can be worn for directional monitoring when discretion is not required.

Technical Video Devices

Technical video devices are similar to standard video cameras, except for their size and how they are employed. Such video devices will not include a videotaping mechanism. All images received will be transmitted to a receiver in a technical observation post, where the taping will be conducted. Technical video devices are normally equipped with a technical listening device, or they are used in conjunction with a separate listening device. As with lis-tening devices, video devices will involve either wire or wireless transmissions, reflecting relatively the same advantages and disadvantages. Wire transmissions invariably provide higher resolution than wireless. Power considerations for video devices are the same as those for listening devices. Video devices are normally mounted behind a wall with a pinhole lens that images through a small, nail-sized hole. The larger the hole, the wider the scope of the image.

Technical Tracking Devices

Technical tracking devices are employed to assist the team in monitoring the movements of the target. This requires that a tracking device be collocated with the target in one form or another. Due to circumstances and access, the most common application of tracking devices is on the vehicle of the target. One example of tracking devices that was developed for monitoring the movements of a target individual is a money case that is used by undercover law enforcement personnel in operations involving money exchanges. The undercover agent will provide the target with money as an element of the operation. The money case used will be equipped with a tracking device, which will assist the surveillance element in monitoring the movements of the target after the meeting is completed. Surveillance teams, however, will rarely have the opportunity to place a tracking device directly with the target. Additionally, tracking devices are expensive and will rarely be employed if the probability of payoff is not high.

A tracking capability allows the surveillance team to monitor the general activities of the target without exposing surveillance vehicles during extended periods of travel. When the target stops or travels to a location of operational interest, the team can be directed to that location and concentrate its effort accordingly.

Standard tracking devices are compact and can be surreptitiously attached to a vehicle. The operator who attaches the device must be aware of the propagation specifications in order to attach the device in a location that will yield the greatest transmission range while minimizing the probability of detection. The tracking device will transmit a signal to a receiver, which is used to monitor the movement of the target. The receiver should be equipped with a visual 360-degree display of relative bearing, a motion status indicator to inform the team when the target is moving, and a distance indicator to inform the team of how far the target is from the receiver.

The distance indicator is an important specification because when the transmitter is out of range from the receiver, the signal is unreadable and the tracking device serves no purpose to the team. When this occurs there will normally be only one surveillance vehicle with the receiver, making it the only one with the capability to search for the beacon signal. When possible, it is ideal to have an aircraft equipped with the receiver, because it is easier for an aircraft to maintain pace with the target or to search an area for a lost signal. Additionally, there are infrared beacons that can be emplaced and that are ideal for aircraft monitoring.

MISCELLANEOUS SURVEILLANCE EQUIPMENT

The amount of equipment that a surveillance team can use in support of an operation is limitless. Miscellaneous equipment can range from hang-gliders to scuba gear. Since much of the specialized equipment is situation dependent and not acquired for standard use, it is neither necessary nor practical to attempt to touch upon them all. There are, however, some basic miscellaneous equipment capabilities that warrant discussion.

Bicycles

A surveillance team should maintain a fleet of common-model bicycles for use in special situations. Bicycles can be very effective in maintaining command of a target vehicle when travelling through dense downtown traffic. In such circumstances it is very difficult for the team to make up any distance on the target. Rush-hour traffic will make it difficult for a surveillance vehicle to regain command of the target if caught behind a traffic light. Bicycles can easily maneuver around traffic obstacles that are insurmountable to a vehicle. Bicycles can also be very effective in supporting foot operators in areas where surveillance vehicles are unable to traverse and provide support.

Paper and Pencils, Tape Recorders

Sufficient note pads and pencils should be available in each of the surveillance vehicles to make written notes of their observations of the target's actions. Tape recorders are commonly used by surveillance operators who are driving by themselves and unable to make written notes of the target's activities. In some courts of law, tape-recorded observations stand as more credible evidence than written notes. Tape recorders should be miniature voice-activated models. (Chapter 9 will address how a tape recorder can be used to decipher a previously dialed number from a public telephone.)

Aircraft

Aircraft provide an equipment capability that can significantly enhance the effectiveness of a surveillance operation. The use of aircraft in support of physical surveillance operations is a standard practice for national agencies such as the FBI. Fixed-wing and rotary-wing aircraft are both suitable for surveillance operations. Fixed-wing aircraft, such as twin-engine planes, are less expensive to purchase, rent, and maintain than helicopters. Helicopters have more flexibility to land in locations other than established airstrips, but this is rarely a discriminating requirement for a surveillance operation unless an apprehension is involved.

The aircraft used should be equipped with a communications system that will integrate with the surveillance team's communications network like those of any of the surveillance vehicles. Aircraft are particularly valuable on long highway or rural follows. This capability allows the surveillance vehicles to lie back and minimize their exposure while the aircraft commands the target. The aircraft will inform the team of significant movements of the target, allowing the team to concentrate its effort at the appropriate time. An aircraft is also a valuable capability when the team is employing an electronic or infrared tracking device.

4

SURVEILLANCE
OPERATION
PREPARATION

A surveillance operation is a comprehensive effort, the success of which depends on a number of interrelated factors. The previous chapters addressed the importance of operator skills and surveillance equipment. Subsequent to this chapter, the book will be dedicated to the tactics that integrate the entire effort. This chapter will address how a surveillance team evaluates the resources of equipment, manpower, and tactical proficiency to prepare for an operation effectively and efficiently.

A surveillance operation is a complicated effort, requiring thorough preparation to minimize uncertainty and error. The better prepared the team is, the greater its chances of success. As a surveillance team progresses with a surveillance operation, it gains confidence and security based on its enhanced understanding of the target. At the beginning of the operation, however, this insight does not exist. As a result, the team is extremely vulnerable to unanticipated actions by the target.

Additionally, the target tends to be extremely observant of his surroundings when departing his residence. Since much of the operation will focus on the target's residence, this adds another dimension of vulnerability to the surveillance team. Meticulous preparation is the primary means of minimizing these and other initial vulnerability factors.

Every single surveillance operation is unique to some degree. The target, terrain, and operational objectives will differ from one operation to another. In preparation for a surveillance operation, the team will examine these factors to determine how its resources can be employed optimally against a given target.

The two primary factors in preparing for a surveillance operation are the target and the objectives of the operation. The operational objectives will be determined by the agency that employs the surveillance team. Normally, surveillance is used as an investigative tool to support the overall objectives of an investigation. The types of investigative objectives and derivative surveillance objectives are limitless. They can consist of the development of evidence for legal prosecution or other purposes, the identification of operational activity, the development of investigative leads to include the identification of contacts of the target, or the development of exploitable information regarding the target, which can be used as leverage against him in interrogation or negotiation.

INFORMATION ASSESSMENT

At the initiation of the preparation phase, the entire surveillance team must be thoroughly briefed on all previously developed information regarding the target. The amount of information that the investigation has developed on a given target will determine the amount of preparation necessary. This may also limit the amount of preparation that is possible.

Given the objectives of the surveillance operation, the minimum information necessary to conduct an effective operational preparation consists of the following:

• *Identifying Data*. Regarding the target, identifying data consists of information that will assist the team in identifying the target when the operation begins. At a minimum, this must include photographs and a detailed description of the target. When this is not available, the team may mount a limited surveillance to obtain photographs of the target for planning purposes. Other types of identifying data will include the target's residence, dress, and mannerisms.

• *Type of Transportation.* This information consists of the mode of transportation that the target is expected to use during the course of the surveillance. At a minimum, this will include a full description of all vehicles owned or used by the target, to include license numbers. If the team does not have an actual picture of the target vehicle, it should go to a car dealership to obtain pictures of a vehicle that is identical to that of the target's. Pictures should be taken from all angles to give the entire team a good image of the vehicle it must identify and follow. Any other identifying features, such as dents, bumper stickers, and modifications, should also be identified for planning purposes. If the target does not own a vehicle, this will be a significant factor in the team's preparation, making the research of public transportation in the operational area a higher priority. This may also require that the team obtain descriptions or photographs of vehicles owned by the target's associates.

• *Patterns and Habits.* Information regarding the target's patterns and habits will depend on the degree of information previously developed on the target. Such information will consist of where the target works, his work hours, his financial status, his hobbies and social interests, his associates and their residences, his relatives and their residences, and frequented establishments.

An important aspect that may appear obvious but should not be taken lightly is the reason that the surveillance team is tasked to follow a target. Recall that in Chapter 1 the types of surveillance targets were discussed. The illegal or operational activity that the target is known or alleged to be involved in is a key indicator as to which category of target he may be. Determining whether the target has had training in surveillance countermeasures or whether he may be surveillance conscious are key factors in how the preparation and subsequent operation are conducted. This determination will also involve an assessment of how dangerous a target may be in confrontational situations. This has an impact on whether the team will carry firearms, if this is not already a standard practice. The examination of the target's activities should include identified methods of operation practiced by the target during the conduct of his illegal or operational activities. If these have not been identified, the team should examine general methods of operation that are common to the alleged illegal or operational activities of the target.

When there is insufficient information regarding the target's patterns and habits, the team may choose to conduct a limited surveillance of the target with the objective of developing adequate information to prepare for the formal surveillance operation. When this is the case, the surveillance team will conduct a "loose" surveillance for a period of one to two weeks to determine general patterns and habits of the target. This does not necessarily support the actual objectives of the investigation; rather, it establishes a basis from which to thoroughly prepare for the surveillance operation.

DETERMINE OPERATIONAL AREA

When the surveillance team is confident that there is sufficient information from which to plan the operation, the actual preparation phase will begin. This is initiated by determining the parameters of the anticipated operational area. The operational area is the area in which the team anticipates the surveillance operation to be primarily based. This will normally be centered around the target's residence and will include the target's workplace when applicable.

The team will further examine the information available from the patterns and habits category discussed previously. From this, the team will determine significant locations to which the target may be expected to travel during the course of the operation. Once again, this may include the residences of relatives within convenient travelling distance, the residences of known associates, and establishments the target is known to frequent. The parameters of the operational area are not determined to restrict the surveillance operation—rather, to focus the team's preparation efforts. When the operational area has been identified, the team will acquire sufficient mapping of the area. Maps will be selected based on the specifications discussed in the previous chapter. Mapping should cover a much larger area than the anticipated operational area because the surveillance will obviously continue wherever the target travels. The maps should be prepared with dots for operational efficiency. If the road maps do not include identification of public transportation systems, then supplemental mapping of this should be acquired.

As the mapping is being acquired, the team will determine the equipment necessary to support the objectives of the operation. Equipment that is not already organic to the team will be acquired and the necessary training in its use conducted. Surveillance vehicles will be prepared with communications equipment and inspected for maintenance and safety. The team will determine the basic issue of equipment for each surveillance vehicle and each operator.

When the mapping of the area is available, the team will conduct a map reconnaissance (recon) of the operational area. It will identify the locations of the target's residence, workplace, associates' and relatives' residences, and establishments he may visit. Based on this, the team will determine the likely routes the target will use throughout the operational area. When this is complete, the team will be given recon assignments. The purpose of this is for team members to conduct a thorough examination of a given location or area in order to identify all aspects that will impact on the surveillance operation.

Some team members will conduct a recon of a specific location, such as the target's residence or workplace. Others will conduct a general recon of a given area primarily to determine traffic patterns. A recon of the public transportation system in the area will be conducted. Of course, if the target is expected to use public transportation as a primary mode of transportation, this recon will be very thorough. In addition to the specific areas or locations that are to be examined, each recon should include observations regarding the following:

• *General Populace.* Observations regarding the race, ethnic background, customs, and language of the general populace in the operational area are important in preparing for an operation. Knowledge of cultural and religious aspects of the populace may also impact on the operation. In addition to these aspects, the team should determine the average class status in regard to the type of clothes worn and the type of vehicles driven in the area. Such observations will assist the team in determining the most appropriate operators to use in certain situations, the type of dress that the team should employ, and the type of vehicles that the team should use in order to blend with the surrounding populace.

• *Law Enforcement Presence.* The degree to which a given operational area is patrolled by law enforcement personnel will impact on the team's planning. If the area has a high crime rate, this alone should stand as a strong indication that law enforcement presence will be regular. Police precincts or stations in the area are another indicator. Law enforcement personnel detect suspicious activity for a living. The very presence of such personnel in the operational area increases the possibility of the team being exposed. A policeman who approaches a surveillance vehicle or operator in the line of duty may draw the target's attention to the surveillance effort. The team should also attempt to observe how strictly traffic and other law violations are enforced. When law enforcement presence is anticipated to be significant, the team should coordinate with the local authorities if appropriate. Additional factors impacting on law enforcement presence will be addressed in the next chapter.

• *General Traffic Patterns.* While team members are conducting their recons, they should continuously examine the general traffic patterns in the operational area. In any given area, individuals who are aware of the traffic patterns will know the areas that are busy and should be avoided. Through such observations the team may be able to anticipate alternative routes available to the target, who will also be familiar with the traffic patterns in the area. Built-up areas or construction zones are examples of areas that may have an impact on the travel patterns of the target and would not be obvious through the initial map recon. The team should also observe traffic characteristics to ensure that when the operation is ongoing, the team drives its surveillance vehicles in a manner that blends with surrounding traffic. For example, if double parking is standard and not enforced in the operational area, the team may be able to do the same when necessary without appearing conspicuous.

TARGET RESIDENCE RECON

The recon of the target's residence is probably the most important of the operation. The team should know the target's work hours to minimize the possibility of the target being home when the recon is conducted. Regardless of whether the target is assumed to be home or not, the recon should be conducted in a manner that would appear natural to any observers. An initial evaluation of the target's ability to observe through his windows and out onto the streets will provide the team an idea of how readily their activities outside of the residence can be observed by the target. The team will conduct their recon accordingly and will certainly employ this information during the actual conduct of the surveillance operation.

When the target lives in a house, the recon should begin by identifying the number of entrances and exits to the residence. The team will then determine the most likely location for the target to park his vehicle. Based on this information, the team can deduce the most likely route by which the target will depart his residence and walk to his vehicle. Given this deduction, the team will identify possible locations where surveillance vehicles or operators can position themselves discreetly to observe the target when he departs his residence and enters his vehicle. For most residences this is a very simple process. If the target parks his vehicle in an enclosed garage, then obviously the garage door will be the focal point.

Next the team will identify the vehicular routes of travel that the target may use when departing his residence. As will be discussed in the next chapter on stakeouts, this will have a direct bearing on where the surveillance vehicles are positioned when the target is in his residence. The team will identify traffic obstacles such as traffic lights, which may impact on the team's ability to pick up the target. They will then identify the most likely routes that the target will use to travel to primary routes of travel throughout the operational area. There will normally be a number of such routes identified. Emphasis will be dedicated to examining the primary routes to the target's workplace and other residences and establishments to which the target is expected to travel.

In conducting a recon of the target's residence, the team will also identify such establishments as markets, restaurants, and stores that the target may travel to by foot. The possible routes which the target may take from his residence to these locations will be examined to anticipate any obstacles the team may encounter when conducting a foot surveillance to those locations. The inside of such establishments should be studied to ensure that there is sufficient cover for operators to enter behind the target if necessary.

The team will also identify public transportation within walking distance of the target's residence. Locations such as taxi stands, bus stops, and subway stations within walking distance should be examined to determine how the team should react if the target walks to these locations. This information will be provided to the members of the team who are conducting a thorough recon of the area's public transportation system.

If the target lives in an apartment, the team must determine the exact location of the target's unit and the windows to that unit that can be observed from the surrounding area. This examination will also assess the target's ability to observe outside activity. Apartment buildings will normally have more entrances and exits for use by the target. The team must identify all of these and then determine the most likely ones to be used by the target based on the location of his apartment unit. If there is designated parking for the apartment complex residents, then the team must determine the location of the target's designated space. When the team is not this fortunate, it must attempt to deduce which portion of the parking area will likely be used by the target.

If a sound deduction cannot be made based on available information, the team may select to break security and conduct a limited recon of the apartment complex when the target is home to identify the location used by the target for parking. It is important that this location be identified because it will be a key indication as to the route the target will travel when departing the apartment complex. Given this information, the team will then identify the possible routes of travel away from the apartment complex, in a manner similar to the methods previously discussed. The recon of a hotel in which a target resides will be similar to that of an apartment complex.

The recon procedures previously discussed may appear to be

extreme preparation for what may be a very simple evaluation. This detail in planning is justified, however, because any information that minimizes the surveillance team's initial uncertainty and vulnerability will enhance the probability of success. This detail in planning is required in all phases of operational preparation.

TARGET WORKPLACE RECON

A recon of the target's workplace is conducted to determine how the team will cover the target when he departs for the day. Rarely will the objectives of an operation include a surveillance of the target in the workplace. It is difficult for a surveillance team to operate in an enclosed work area for any period of time without detection. Normally, if the investigative agency needs information regarding the target while at work, it will recruit a source who works close enough to the target to make observations. Other options are to place an undercover agent in the workplace or to install technical monitoring devices in the target's immediate work area.

Much of the recon of the workplace can be conducted after work hours, but some portions will have to be conducted while the target is there. For this reason, it is important initially to attempt to determine the target's exact office so that the recon team is aware of which windows are available to the target for outside observation. This informs the team which areas outside of the target's office can be readily observed and should be avoided. This awareness and practice will continue through the recon and into the actual surveillance operation. The team will then note all of the entrances and exits to the workplace and attempt to determine the exit the target will use when departing the building. This information should be developed for contingency purposes, but may not necessarily support the actual surveillance operation. This is the case since the team's objectives will not include following the target while in the workplace; identifying where the target parks and where he exits the parking area should be sufficient. The larger the facility and the work force at the target's workplace, the more difficult this determination will be.

Limited open parking availability around the workplace may indicate that the target's parking patterns will vary daily. When there are many different parking areas the target could possibly use, the team may attempt to identify where the target parks his vehicle. When this information is either deduced or confirmed, the team will determine locations where a surveillance vehicle can be positioned to observe the target vehicle when the actual operation begins. The team will then determine the possible routes by which the target may exit the parking area and enter roads. Based on this information, the team will identify all the possible routes the target may use in departing the area. The team will concentrate on all possible routes while giving particular examination to the most logical routes which the target will use to travel from the workplace to his residence.

The one portion of the recon that must be conducted during work hours may answer all the issues regarding the target's departure activities previously discussed. It is important that the team monitor the traffic from the target's workplace at the end of the workday. This is particularly important if there is a large work force that leaves the area at the same time each day. The team must monitor the traffic to observe how it flows and to identify any traffic obstacles the team may encounter. If the target is observed departing during this portion of the recon, the team has a good indication of which route the target will depart by when the surveillance begins.

SUPPLEMENTAL TEAM RECONS

At least one recon team will examine the primary routes of travel through, and out of, the operational area. This will include a very thorough examination of the traffic patterns that may impact on the routes the target selects to travel. The team will also identify traffic obstacles to include construction zones and built-up areas. This will also include the identification of alternative routes the team can use to avoid such areas during the actual operation. The recon will be conducted during all hours of day and night to determine traffic density along certain routes at certain times. Finally, the team will identify primary routes from the operational area to highways, which represent a fast route out of the area. This is important because the team must be able to anticipate when the target intends to travel to a highway; it is critical for the team to have command of the target when entering any high-speed route.

Regardless of whether the target is known to use public transportation, a recon will be conducted of the public transportation system in the city where the target resides. Of course, if the target is known to use public transportation as a primary means, the recon will be much more thorough to reflect this fact. This recon will include ensuring that the team has public transportation routes included in their maps or that supplemental public transportation mapping is acquired. The team should acquire the applicable bus and subway schedules to support the operation. If there is a bus stop or subway station within walking distance of the target's residence or workplace, a recon of these locations should be conducted. The recon of a subway station will be conducted in a manner that supports the tactics of covering a target when he enters a subway station (Chapter 9).

The recon of the subway and bus systems should include determining how use is paid for. This will ensure that the team carries the appropriate change and can purchase subway tickets or pay a bus driver quickly and without drawing undue attention. The team should examine the actual connecting systems involved in both the bus and subway systems. This will allow the team to make a smooth transition when following the target and also to anticipate the target's possible destinations when entering a particular bus or subway line. A recon of main train stations and the primary servicing airport should be conducted as well. The recon of any bus station, subway station, train station, or airport will include checking the quality of communications between surveillance vehicles outside the location and operators inside. Such a recon will also assess the security forces and systems in these locations that may impact on the operation.

Individual recons will be conducted of any establishments or residences of associates or relatives that the target is expected to visit during the operation. The recon of residences will concentrate on how the team will position itself to cover the area when the target is visiting. The recon of public establishments will include an examination of the inside areas to determine if there is sufficient cover for operators to enter behind the target when necessary. The recon will determine how the team can best observe the target if he enters a given establishment, to include checking communications with operators inside the establishment. An examination of the dress and mannerisms of the clientele will be included.

FINAL PREPARATION ACTIVITIES

When all of the necessary recons have been completed, team members will conduct a formal briefing to the entire team and the supported investigative agency, if applicable. This will be a comprehensive briefing of all areas reconned and should include pictures, slides, and drawings. The briefing should thoroughly familiarize each of the team members with all aspects of the individual recons. It will include a detailed explanation of the cover story and any cover documentation that has been acquired to support the operation. If firearms are to be carried on the operation, the rules of engagement and deadly force guidelines will be explained.

At the conclusion of the briefing, the team will make a final evaluation of whether it can effectively support the operation given current funding, manpower, equipment, and preparation. If it has not already been done, the team will determine when and where the operation will begin. If the operation is expected to continue for an extended period, it is normally best to begin during the workweek. During this time the target will normally conform to a standard workweek routine. This allows the team to become familiar with the target's characteristics and patterns with relatively few surprises. It is more difficult for the operation to begin on a weekend because anything could happen then.

Communications procedures should be a standard surveillance team practice. As a final item of preparation, the team should coordinate such communications procedures as brevity codes, radio frequencies, and visual communications signals if body communications equipment will not be used. Each operator should have surveillance vehicle telephone numbers committed to memory or written down for use as appropriate.

If the team intends to use a central control base, the operators should have this telephone number as well. Recontact and rendezvous procedures should be established for operators who lose communications contact with the team.

As the final preparatory action, the surveillance vehicle crewing for the initial phase of the operation will be determined. Surveillance vehicle crewing simply refers to which operators will man a given surveillance vehicle. Each surveillance vehicle, or operator if applicable, will be given a specific assignment for the initial stakeout of the operation. The surveillance chief will tell the team when to be in position for the stakeout, and the preparation will conclude with the team members synchronizing their watches.

SURVEILLANCE
STAKEOUTS

Since this is the first discussion of tactical applications, a general difference in vehicular and foot surveillance will be addressed. Many of the tactics that apply to vehicular surveillance apply equally to foot surveillance. The primary difference is that vehicular surveillance is more of an exact science because it has more standard restrictions. Most of these restrictions affect maneuverability. For example, a foot operator can reverse direction by simply turning around, while a similar maneuver by vehicle is much more complicated.

Another primary restriction is channelized travel because the movement of vehicles is normally restricted by established roadways. Because of these and other factors, the discussion of surveillance tactics must be much more specific in their application to vehicular surveillance. For this reason, because the book discusses tactics common to both vehicular and foot surveillance, they will be addressed in the context of their application to vehicular surveillance. The reader will easily discern how these tactics also apply to foot surveillance.

When the tactic addressed is unique to one of the two methods, this will be specified.

In the previous chapter, some basic principles of team preparation for the initial stakeout were discussed. A *stakeout* is basically a logical positioning of operators or surveillance vehicles to attain initial command of a target who either travels through a specified area or emerges from that area. A *surveillance box* is the positioning of surveillance vehicles or operators in such a manner as to control routes of travel out of a specified area. The most common examples of when a stakeout is employed are 1) when the team expects the target to leave his residence in the morning but has not observed the residence through the night and therefore cannot be certain that the target is at home; 2) when the target is expected to leave work, but the team is not certain which exit he will depart by; or 3) when the target is expected to visit the residence of an acquaintance.

In Chapter 1, the four phases of a surveillance operation were discussed. The stakeout is the first phase of a surveillance operation, and the box is the fourth phase. In Chapter 7 the surveillance-box phase will be discussed in detail. The stakeout and the box employ most of the same tactics.

BOX POSITIONS

The most basic tactic fundamental to both the stakeout and the surveillance box is the use of box positions. These are the actual positions that surveillance vehicles or operators establish to perform their given assignment in controlling a route of travel out of the area being boxed or staked out. The primary box positions are the trigger, the commit, the enter, and the control. These positions are discussed individually here.

Trigger Box Position

The *trigger* is a surveillance vehicle or operator that does not have visual command of the target but is in a position that provides some degree of command. The most common trigger positions are visual observation of a doorway from which the target is expected to exit and a surveillance vehicle with visual observation of the target's vacant vehicle. The degree of command in the latter example is that the target is expected to return to his vehicle eventually. Particularly in situations where the team has lost command of the target, a surveillance box with a trigger surveillance vehicle on the target vehicle is a very effective method of reestablishing command. In some circumstances there may be more than one trigger position in the box. Observation posts, which will be discussed at the conclusion of this chapter, are excellent for use as trigger positions.

Commit Box Position

A *commit* box position is one from which a surveillance vehicle or operator can observe the target at a specified point and determine the target's direction of travel from that point. Although a commit surveillance vehicle can inform the team as to the target's direction of travel, if it is only in a commit position it will be unable to assume immediate command of the target through a pickup and a follow.

Enter Box Position

An *enter* box position is one that allows a surveillance vehicle or operator to initiate a follow along a specified route of travel and establish command of the target prior to a specified point. Although an enter surveillance vehicle is positioned to maneuver for command of the target after passing through a specified location, it cannot observe the target as he passes through that location. If a surveillance vehicle is only an enter, it must have a commit surveillance vehicle covering the same point to inform the enter vehicle when the target has passed the specified location. This in effect informs the enter surveillance vehicle to pull out and initiate a follow.

Control Box Position

A *control* box position is one that allows a surveillance vehicle or operator to perform both the commit and enter assignments as described above. A control can observe the target as it reaches a specified point and maneuver to establish command after the target passes that point. When terrain permits, it is ideal for a surveillance vehicle to establish a control position when developing the box. This allows one surveillance vehicle to complete an assignment that would otherwise require two.

PICKUP

Once again, a stakeout box is established when there is no visual command of the target, but the target is expected to pass through or emerge from within a specified area being boxed. In the stakeout, surveillance vehicles establish their box positions in order to cover all routes out of a specified area. This ensures that when the target enters or emerges from within the box, the team will pick up the target as he exits the box. The pickup begins when the target is first observed either entering the box or emerging from within the box. The follow begins when the target exits the stakeout box and the appropriate surveillance vehicle attains visual command of the target while he is moving.

Figure 1 depicts a stakeout box that has been established in anticipation that the target will pass through a specified intersection. The five surveillance vehicles (Alpha, Bravo, Charlie, Delta, and Echo) are depicted in simplified positions to illustrate the point. Surveillance vehicles Alpha, Bravo, Charlie, and Delta are all positioned in control box assignments on different routes of travel. Each of these four surveillance vehicles can commit the target into the box and control out of the box. Notice that all four routes into and out of the stakeout box are covered. Surveillance vehicle Echo is in position to commit the intersection.

Figure 2 illustrates the dynamics of the stakeout box as the target enters the box from the east travelling west. As the target passes surveillance vehicle Charlie's position, Charlie commits him into the box by transmitting the information to the entire team. At this point all surveillance vehicles, including Charlie, will remain in place. As the target turns right at the intersection, surveillance vehicle Echo commits the target by informing the team that the target has turned right and is travelling north. Once again, all surveillance vehicles will remain stationary. As the target passes surveillance vehicle Bravo's position, Bravo commits the target by informing the team that the target is still travelling north. At this point the target has broken the box, so the rest of the team will leave their positions and maneuver to support the follow. At the appropriate time, Bravo will pull out and enter to establish command of the target. As Bravo establishes command of the target, the surveillance has progressed from the pickup phase to the follow phase.

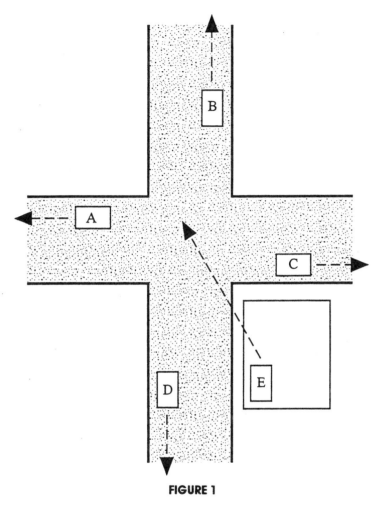

FIGURE 1

It is important to note that the surveillance vehicles do not leave their box positions until the target has exited, or broken, the box. This is key because after the target enters the stakeout box, he can conduct any number of maneuvers, to include stopping or turning around. In such circumstances, a surveillance vehicle that maneuvers from its box position prematurely may expose itself unnecessarily or leave a hole in the box through which the target may depart undetected.

Figure 3 depicts a stakeout box that has been established in anticipation that the target will emerge from within a specified area. The six surveillance vehicles (Alpha, Bravo, Charlie,

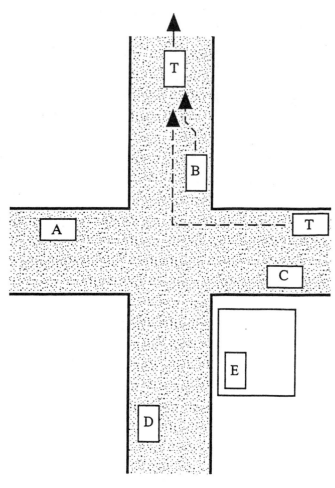

FIGURE 2

Delta, Echo, and Golf) are depicted in simplified positions. Surveillance vehicles Alpha, Bravo, Charlie, Delta, and Echo are all positioned on different routes of travel in control assignments. Notice that all routes of travel from the box are covered. Surveillance vehicle Golf is positioned to trigger the parking garage exit from which the target vehicle is expected to emerge.

Figure 4 depicts the dynamics of the stakeout box as the target emerges. As the target vehicle exits the garage, Golf triggers the pickup by informing the team of the target's activity. As the target

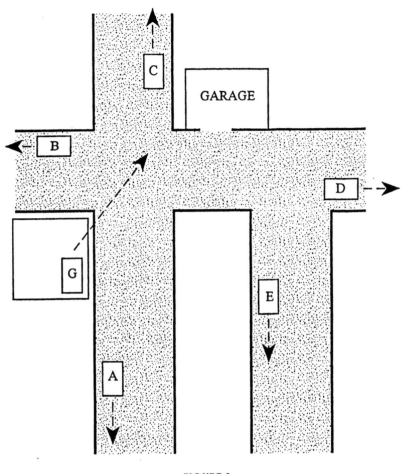

FIGURE 3

turns left onto the street, Golf commits the target east by once again informing the team. As the target turns right to travel south, either Delta or Echo may be in position to commit the turn at the intersection. If not, little command is lost because Echo is in position to commit the target south as it passes Echo's box position. As the target passes, Echo will commit by informing the team that the target is travelling south on the specified road.

At this point the box has been broken, and the remaining surveillance vehicles will maneuver to support the follow. At the appropriate

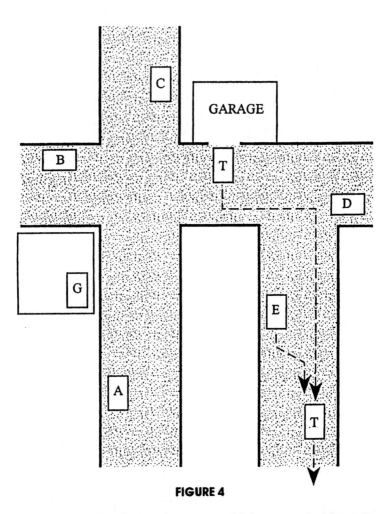

FIGURE 4

instant, Echo will pull out and enter to establish command of the target.

Figure 5 once again depicts a stakeout box established in anticipation of the target emerging from within a specified area around a parking garage. All six surveillance vehicles are positioned in control assignments covering each route of travel out of the box. Since there are six routes that must be covered and only six surveillance vehicles available, the team must forgo the luxury of a trigger. This requires that all surveillance vehicles maintain an increased degree of awareness.

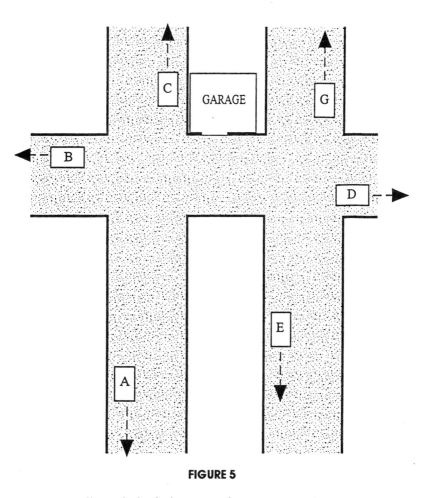

FIGURE 5

Regardless of which direction the target travels, none of the surveillance vehicles will observe the target until the box is broken along one of the routes. The pickup and follow will begin as one of the surveillance vehicles commits and enters to assume command of the target.

REINFORCING BOX POSITIONS

A reinforcing box position is employed when all the routes of travel out of the stakeout box are covered and there are one or more surveillance vehicles in addition to those required for the basic box. In such situations, additional surveillance vehicles will look ahead and assess the terrain to determine which routes have traffic obstacles or traffic hazards that could jeopardize a successful pickup and follow. Traffic obstacles include traffic lights, toll roads, dense traffic, or construction zones that could impede the progress of a successful surveillance follow after the pickup. Any additional surveillance vehicle can be positioned beyond a traffic obstacle to continue the follow in the event that a boxing surveillance vehicle is impeded by that obstacle.

Traffic hazards are options that afford the target a number of avenues from which to escape quickly, such as a highway intersection by vehicle or a subway station by foot. If the target is not under command when he enters the traffic hazard, the surveillance effort will have a difficult time reestablishing command of the target and will certainly degrade team integrity in the effort. (This degradation to team integrity will be better understood after the discussion of lost command drills in Chapter 7.) The team may choose to position any additional surveillance vehicles ahead on the route(s) leading to traffic hazards to ensure that command is established if the target travels to that hazard. As the reader employs these principles on the road, the importance of reinforcing box positions will become readily apparent.

Figure 6 depicts a variation of the last two stakeout examples. In this example, since the initial route of travel is a one-way street, only four surveillance vehicles are necessary to establish the stakeout box. Surveillance vehicles Alpha, Bravo, and Charlie are in control positions along their designated routes of travel. Surveillance vehicle Delta is positioned as a trigger. This leaves surveillance vehicles Echo and Golf to employ in reinforcing box positions. Since there is a traffic light that represents a traffic obstacle along surveillance vehicle Bravo's designated route, surveillance vehicle Echo is positioned in a reinforcing control position along that route. Note that Echo is positioned beyond the traffic obstacle in order to establish command of the target if he travels through the traffic light and Bravo is stopped. Since there is a highway that represents a traffic hazard to the north of surveillance vehicle Alpha's designated route, surveillance vehicle Golf is

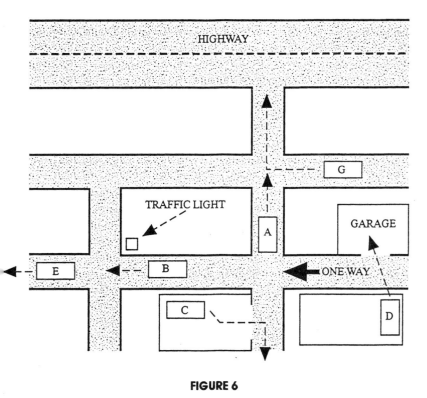

FIGURE 6

in a reinforcing control position to establish command of the target prior to the hazard in case Alpha is unable to do so.

SURVEILLANCE VEHICLE BOX POSITIONING

The previous discussions moved directly from the definition of each of the box positions to their basic tactical application in the stakeout and pickup. Now the discussion will digress to a more detailed explanation of box positions. It is one accomplishment to be able to box an assignment, but the professional operator must employ tactical knowledge in selecting a position to ensure that the assignment can be completed while maintaining cover from the target.

Trigger Positioning
There are a number of considerations that must be exercised

when selecting the trigger position. Initially, the trigger must assess the most likely route the target will take when exiting a location on foot or the most likely direction from which he will travel when approaching his vehicle. With this assessment made, the trigger surveillance vehicle will position itself in a location that ensures observation of the target while minimizing possible exposure.

If a position cannot be established that virtually ensures that the target will not walk past the surveillance vehicle, the stakeout box should be established without a trigger. The target is always more observant when departing his residence or his workplace. Always remember that one of the greatest risks to the security of an operation is that the target may walk by and look inside a surveillance vehicle. If the target confronts a surveillance operator or vehicle, the operation is severely compromised for obvious reasons.

A trigger on a door should be established in a position away from the direction the target will travel as he departs. The trigger of the target vehicle should be established in a position away from the direction by which the target will approach his vehicle. This position should also be out of the line of sight of the target as he observes traffic to pull out and travel away. Additionally, the target will have a tendency to observe his surroundings as he unlocks his vehicle. The trigger should be positioned to avoid casual observation from the target at this point as well.

When the trigger observes the target departing the area, it should stay in place, following the principle of not maneuvering until the target breaks the box. This is also a point at which the target will be very observant of his surroundings. In addition to observing surrounding traffic to negotiate his own way, the target will be more aware of vehicles that appear to pull out and react to his movements. This is also a primary point at which countersurveillance, if present, will concentrate. In any case, if the stakeout box is properly applied the trigger should not be needed to initiate the follow.

Commit Positioning

Commit positions are normally selected when it is critical to the success of a pickup that a specific location, such as an intersection, be committed. Ideally, a surveillance vehicle will establish a control box position at the location, but this is not always possible. In such situations, the commit should take advantage of the fact that it is not expected to enter. This provides the surveillance vehicle flexibility in establishing a commit position that is well covered or completely concealed. Since the surveillance vehicle is not expected to maneuver for command of the target initially, it is rarely necessary to be in a position that is in the direct line of sight of the target as he passes the specified location. Every effort should be made to establish commit positions off the main routes of travel. Parking lots normally provide excellent cover for commit surveillance vehicles. Foot operators can commit either the target or the target vehicle from inside shops or restaurants by positioning themselves in a good position to look out of a window.

Enter Positioning

A box position that is solely an enter will always be used in conjunction with a commit surveillance vehicle at the same location. The reasoning here is simple: for the enter vehicle to know when to pull out and maneuver for command of the target, another surveillance vehicle must be able to see the target. The commit surveillance vehicle will inform the enter surveillance vehicle, as well as the rest of the team, when the target passes the designated location.

Based on this information, the enter surveillance vehicle will pull out and maneuver to establish command of the target. This, however, is an inefficient use of surveillance vehicles in the overall team concept because it requires two surveillance vehicles to accomplish an assignment that would ideally be performed by one. This tactic is necessary, however, at critical options or intersections that are not suitable for a single control vehicle. This arrangement is often necessary at highway interchanges or highway overpasses.

Provided that a surveillance vehicle is able to complete a commit assignment at the specified location, the enter surveillance vehicle must follow some basic rules in selecting a position. First, enter positions will always be off of the main route that the target is expected to travel. Obviously, if the surveillance vehicle is parked on the main route of travel, it would also be able to commit. When selecting an enter position, the surveillance vehicle must ensure that it can make an unimpeded entry onto the main route of travel. The two most common obstacles that impede entry are traffic and traffic lights. The traffic light obstacle is easy to overcome—do not select an avenue of entry that has a traffic light at the anticipated main route of travel. In areas or locations that allow right turns on red this may not be as significant a problem, unless the enter surveillance vehicle is stopped behind another vehicle that does not intend to turn right.

To lower the probability of traffic impeding entry, positioning should be based on the traffic flow expected on the main route of travel. On two-way roads, the enter surveillance vehicle should always select a position that allows it to enter the main route of travel from the right side as the traffic flows. This ensures that the enter surveillance vehicle can make a right turn onto the main route rather than a left turn. Making a left turn disproportionately increases the difficulty in entering the main route because the surveillance vehicle is impeded by traffic travelling in both directions. On one-way roads this applies to a lesser degree. Although the probability of impeding traffic from the road to be entered is the same from either side, a surveillance vehicle attempting a left turn onto a one-way road may still be impeded by oncoming traffic. These are important considerations, but they can be employed less rigidly in residential or rural areas where traffic is light and presents a negligible obstacle.

Figure 7 depicts a simple scenario involving a commit surveillance vehicle (Alpha) in conjunction with an enter surveillance vehicle (Bravo).

Surveillance vehicle Alpha is positioned in a parking lot that provides a good view of the intersection to be committed. Bravo is positioned off a road that leads to the entry ramp to the target's anticipated main route of travel. As the target passes through the intersection and Alpha commits him past the entry ramp, Bravo maneuvers to establish command of the target.

Control Positioning
The most basic positioning for a control position is for the

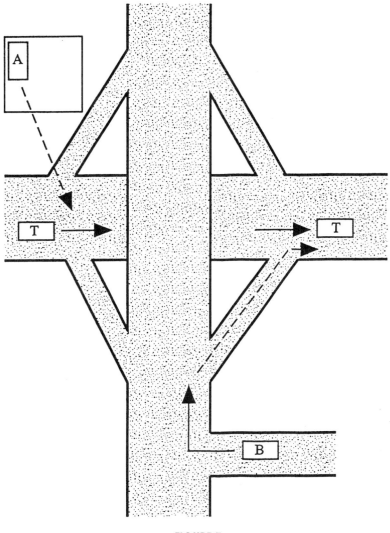

FIGURE 7

surveillance vehicle to parallel park on the right side of the road
on which the target vehicle may pass (Figure 8).

Although this position guarantees a high probability that the
surveillance vehicle can successfully commit and enter to establish command of the target, such a position should be avoided
when possible. The reason for this is that such positioning will
give the target a good look at the surveillance vehicle, at an angle

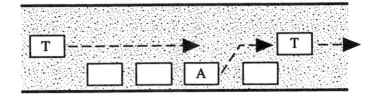

FIGURE 8

that may allow him to see that the surveillance vehicle is manned. Additionally, such a position may appear more suspicious as the surveillance vehicle pulls out after the target passes. This is not to say that positions on the side of the road are a significant risk to security. When there is sufficient cover from other vehicles parked on the side of the road, such positions can be both secure and effective. It is simply a general rule that these positions be avoided when more secure yet equally effective positions are available. When no other option exists, the surveillance vehicle should ensure that the box security precautions discussed later in this chapter are strictly applied.

The best control positions are those that can be established off the main road of travel. Such positions allow the surveillance vehicle to complete the assignment without being in the target's line of sight as he passes by. In selecting these positions, some general rules should be considered. Most important, the surveillance vehicle must be able to observe the commit location. Obviously, if the surveillance vehicle is unable to see the target as he passes, for whatever reason, the enter capability is academic because the target will pass undetected.

Parking lots are often suitable locations for control positioning. The most common and readily available locations for control positions are roads that run perpendicular to and join the main road of travel. By parallel parking on such roads, the surveillance vehicle can observe its designated commit location and enter to establish command of the target (Figure 9). Remember that control positions in parking lots and on perpendicular roads must provide an unimpeded right turn onto the road on which the target is expected to travel, as discussed in the previous section regarding enter positions.

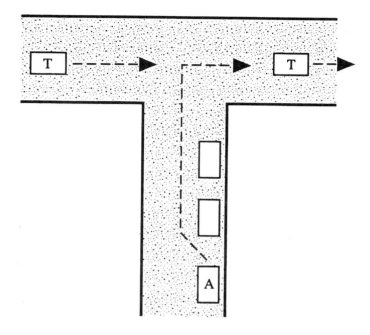

FIGURE 9

Lay-up Position

A *lay-up position* is the last of the options selected when in box positions. A lay-up is an alternative position that a surveillance vehicle may use to avoid staying in its primary box position for too long. A lay-up is only employed when there is a trigger surveillance vehicle to initiate the pickup. This allows the surveillance vehicle to avoid drawing attention to its primary box position by moving to an alternative location. The only rule is that a lay-up position must be selected that will allow the surveillance vehicle to return to its primary box position and accomplish its assignment after receiving the initial alert from the trigger.

BOX POSITION SELECTION

There are a number of considerations that influence the selection of box positions. These are important because, during the stakeout phase, the surveillance team may be required to stakeout the same location or area for hours or even days, waiting for the target to appear. This is the phase in which the team is most vulnerable and susceptible to detection because it is required to maintain basically static positions for long periods.

The very nature of the stakeout dictates a degree of uncertainty and vulnerability because the team is never sure of when or where the target may first appear. Additionally, the stakeout will normally take place in a primary operational area in which the team will be expected to operate for the duration of the operation. For these and other such reasons, it is important that the team select box positions that minimize the probability of its coming to the attention of the target, countersurveillance, police, security forces, or the general populace. This must be done, of course, while at the same time maximizing the probability of successfully completing its box assignments in the pickup of the target.

Cover for Action

The primary consideration in selecting a box position is that there must be a plausible reason—or *cover for action*—for being in a given location. This is necessary so as to blend in with the surroundings to avoid drawing attention. In every situation, a plausible explanation, or cover story, for presence in a given location must be ready to satisfy any inquisition. This can be difficult at times, particularly in rural, residential, or exclusive neighborhoods where the residents and police are familiar with who belongs and who appears alien.

Highly trafficked areas, such as commercial cities, are much more favorable in providing cover for action under which the team can blend. Whatever the case, operators must select positions with sufficient cover or employ resourcefulness in establishing their own cover for action: When undue interest of the target or a third party is noted, surveillance operators should not make any unusual actions or leave immediately unless absolutely necessary. Such actions only enhance suspicion and increase the probability that the target will become more observant or that the authorities will be notified. In such circumstances, the operators should take actions that provide a plausible reason for presence before departing in a natural manner.

Security Forces/Police

When a surveillance operation is conducted without the knowledge of the local law enforcement agencies, such elements pose a significant risk to its security and effectiveness. The following are factors that must be considered when choosing box positions:

- *Proximity of Police Stations.* Obviously there will be a disproportionate number of police personnel travelling through an area near a police station. Although many of these personnel are not actually on duty, police are observant by nature. This significantly enhances the possibility of detection. Even if the team can provide the authorities with a plausible reason for being in the area, or establish the legitimacy of the surveillance operation, once the police are aware of activity in their area they become increasingly active in identifying surveillance operators. They may also be interested in determining the target of the operation. Whether friend or foe, this degrades the overall security of the operation.
- *Crime Rate.* Police, security forces, and in many cases the general populace are normally more suspicious of unusual activity in areas with high crime rates. In such areas, police tend to be less willing to recognize an individual's right to privacy in confronting suspicious activity. Additionally, police will be more responsive to even minor reports from residents. These factors significantly increase the possibility that a surveillance team will be confronted and exposed.
- *Upper-Class Residential Areas.* As with high-crime-rate areas, police are generally more responsive to alerts in upper-class residential areas. Additionally, it can be difficult and expensive for a surveillance team to blend into such areas.
- *Rural or Residential Areas.* As stated previously, rural and residential areas provide little cover because, normally, the only traffic passing through is local to that area. This makes it easier for the target, the police, or the general populace to isolate and identify surveillance operators who are alien to that area.
- *Banks and Luxury Stores.* Banks and luxury stores, such as jewelers, are more likely to employ security personnel or systems to identify and deter potential criminals. In areas with such enhanced security awareness, a surveillance effort can easily be

mistaken for criminals casing the location for a burglary if precautions are not taken. The surveillance team must simply be aware of this fact and avoid selecting box positions in sight of such locations

• *Schools*. Particularly in today's environment, the identification of suspicious individuals in the proximity of schools is a high priority for police, teachers, and parents alike. There is no other area in which suspicious activity will be more actively reported and confronted. This is a risk to the security of a surveillance effort that must be recognized and avoided.

BOX POSITION SECURITY PRECAUTIONS

Once a box position has been selected in respect to the appropriate criteria previously discussed, there are general security precautions that the surveillance team must employ to avoid drawing attention.

• *Avoid Looking Like a Surveillance Vehicle*. Avoiding looking like a surveillance vehicle is a principle that encompasses all other precautions. As stated previously, when on stakeout the surveillance team is most vulnerable to detection by the target because the team is never sure when or where he may appear. When a surveillance vehicle remains in a box position, or circulates among box positions, trash tends to accumulate in the vehicle. This will project an unusual appearance to anyone who may happen by. Coffee cups on the dashboard are a dead giveaway for a stakeout. Surveillance operators must make an effort to ensure that the interior of the surveillance vehicle retains a tidy and natural appearance in order to avoid attracting any undue interest. In most cases, the presence of an infant restraining seat in the backseat will give the surveillance vehicle an air of innocence and dissuade many second looks. Obviously, all equipment that may identify the vehicle as a surveillance vehicle must be kept out of the sight of anyone who may approach the vehicle or pass by. Whether the surveillance vehicle actually is an undercover police vehicle or just comes under the suspicion of the local populace as being such, rumor of the operation will circulate through the operational area. Eventually the word may reach the target.

• *Two Men in a Surveillance Vehicle.* There is something about two men sitting together in a car parked on the side of a road that automatically draws suspicion. In fact, intelligence agents are trained to key on this profile because it is the standard manning for a surveillance vehicle. When possible, the surveillance team should man its surveillance vehicles with a male/female crew. This profile is much less suspicious, and if necessary, a plausible cover for action can be immediately established. Another way to avoid the two-male profile is to have one operator wait in a nearby location such as a coffee shop or park. With body communications equipment, the operator on foot can monitor the activity and return to the surveillance vehicle when necessary. One male sitting in the passenger seat as though waiting for the driver to return is much more natural than two males sitting together. If it is not appropriate for one operator to leave the surveillance vehicle given the circumstances of the operation, one operator in the passenger seat and one in the back seat is another option.

• *Avoid Appearing Operational.* Many times, particularly when the pickup is about to commence, surveillance operators will tend to appear and act alerted or hyped. This is common when the adrenaline soars after hours on stakeout. Items as simple as engines running and emitting exhaust may draw the target's attention as he passes. This may cause the target to look back and observe the surveillance vehicle pull out from behind. Seat belts should remain off until after the target passes the box position because belts being used gives the appearance of a vehicle that is about to pull out. Individuals sitting casually in a vehicle for whatever reason do not do so with their seat belts and shoulder straps on. Many people are not aware that when the brake pedal is engaged even when the engine is not running, most vehicles will still display brake lights. This will alert the target to a vehicle parked along the road that is being manned and may give cause for a more thorough examination when passing.

PICKUP (REVISITED)

During the stakeout and the ensuing pickup, it is imperative that the appropriate surveillance vehicle or operator with visual observation of the target relay as much identifying information regarding the target as possible. This should include a complete description of the target if not previously known, the target's dress and mannerisms, and any identifying objects the target is carrying. A description of dress and mannerisms assists the rest of the team in identifying the target as the operation progresses.

If the target is traveling with one or more individuals, complete descriptions must be given of them as well. When he is traveling by vehicle, it should be indicated whether the target is the driver or a passenger. If not previously available, a complete description of the target vehicle, to include license number, should be relayed to the team. Any identifying features of the vehicle—such as dents, bumper stickers, or dealership labels—that may assist the team in distinguishing it from other similar vehicles should be relayed.

Just one final reminder: when the follow is initiated, the initial enter or control surveillance vehicle should make a smooth and discreet transition from its box position to visual command of the target. The rest of the team will maneuver to support the operation as appropriate, employing the tactics of the follow.

OBSERVATION AND LISTENING POSTS

An observation post is a fixed location that allows surveillance operators to maintain constant discreet observation of a specified location. A listening post is a fixed location that is used by a surveillance team to conduct a technical monitoring mission of a specified location. An observation post may be used to conduct a fixed surveillance of a location when no other surveillance assets are involved. The most common application of an observation post is to support a surveillance stakeout. A listening post may also support the stakeout, but it will normally have an additional, more specific information-gathering objective.

The primary advantage of an observation post is that it allows the constant observation of a given location without requiring a surveillance vehicle or operator to be exposed for this purpose. Observation posts are normally located in a position to observe the target's residence or workplace. Recall that a target will normally be more observant of his surroundings when departing his residence or workplace. This makes a trigger surveillance vehicle parked in a position to observe a departing target vulnerable to detection. An observation post can be used to negate this vulnerability. Additionally, an observation post provides surveillance operators cover to employ larger and more stable photography and video equipment.

Observation posts can be established in houses, apartments, offices, or stores that facilitate the observation of a desired location. When the surveillance team is operating under official law enforcement status it will be easier to secure an appropriate location. If the team cannot, or selects not to, secure a location under official auspices, then it must attempt to rent or lease an appropriate location. This may be difficult when the target lives in a house. Many apartment complexes have sufficient vacancies to facilitate an appropriate observation post, but the team must be resourceful in convincing the apartment manager of which is the most desired rental location. Contracting for office or store space should be approached in the same manner.

Particular care must be taken when setting up and manning an observation post. Curtains must be drawn to ensure that no observation from the outside is possible. Camera equipment should be stabilized on a tripod that is offset from the window. A remote cable release for stabilized equipment is essential to minimizing camera motion. By focusing through a small break in the curtains, a telephoto lens will normally provide adequate observation and photographic capability. At night, the room from which the observation is being conducted should remain unlit to minimize the possibility of outside observation or silhouetting.

When an adequate observation post cannot be established in any of the previously discussed locations, a mobile surveillance system or observation post van can be employed. As discussed in Chapter 3, a mobile observation post will normally take the form of a van that blends with other such vehicles in the operational area.

This vehicle, however, will be equipped with the capability to observe and record the surrounding area. By finding an appropriate parking location, the vehicle can be positioned with a good view of the location to be observed. Normally, the observation vehicle will be manned by two operators to ensure 24-hour coverage and to accommodate safety considerations. The van will be inserted into its position by a separate operator who will park the van, lock it, and depart naturally. This is necessary because it projects a natural appearance, as opposed to a vehicle that is parked and remains without anyone ever exiting.

Another type of observation post uses a standard surveillance vehicle with either remotely controlled and monitored camera equipment or an operator in the trunk with an outside visual capability such as an observation device in the keyhole. Obviously, the latter of the two can only serve a short-term purpose. It is effective, however, when the exact location of the activity to be observed/recorded is known. This allows the operator to observe from a much closer position than would be possible without the cover of the surveillance vehicle.

Listening posts do not require the same specifications in site selection as do observation posts. It is ideal, however, if a listening post can serve as an observation post as well. Recall from the discussion of listening devices and telephone monitoring (Chapter 3) that such capabilities are either transmitted by a wire or by signal. Depending on the application, the distance of the listening post from the monitoring capability will be limited by either the length of wire that can be run or the transmission range of the device.

These factors will impact directly on the location of the listening post. The use of directional microphone monitoring is limited further to line of sight. The use of wire-transmitted devices to a listening post is very difficult from a house, but adjoining apartment units or hotel rooms are ideal. Regardless of the application, the listening post must be located in the same general vicinity as the monitoring capability. As with observation posts, a mobile surveillance vehicle can be used as a listening post.

When using a house, apartment, or hotel room as an observation post or listening post, a realistic cover story must be established. This is necessary to deter the curiosity of the landlord or neighbors. Rent or payment should be made in cash or another form that cannot be traced to the surveillance team or an operator. The capability for radio communications with the team is required. A mobile telephone unit should be used if the location does not have commercial telephone service. Whenever the location is left vacant, all equipment should be removed or well hidden and secured. When using a hotel room, the beds and facilities should appear as if they were used, even when they were not.

Tactical observation and listening posts are those that are established outside and use available cover to blend with the surroundings. These can be established in trees, bushes, sewage drains, or foxholes. They can be manned or remotely monitored. There are a number of specialized equipment packages developed for tactical applications. The other possibilities for establishing observation and listening posts are limitless. Another possible type of mobile observation or listening post is a pickup truck with large appliance boxes in the cab. Operators can monitor activity while concealed inside the boxes. Drug enforcement agents regularly use boats and yachts as observation and listening posts.

BASIC VEHICULAR SURVEILLANCE

Vehicular surveillance is the most basic method of mobile surveillance. One may argue that foot surveillance is less complicated, and in many circumstances it is. But due to the nature of vehicular surveillance, more specific tactical applications are employed. With vehicular surveillance the target's travels are primarily channelized along established roadways. On foot the target has much more flexibility to travel in any direction at any time. Traffic obstacles such as traffic lights and dense traffic are not unique to vehicular operations, but they do further restrict the tactics of a vehicular surveillance.

As with any surveillance operation, the most effective key to success is a coordinated team effort relying on sound tactical and technical execution. An adequate surveillance vehicle communications system, as previously discussed (Chapter 3), is vital to a coordinated effort. Such a system allows the team to react based on the information transmitted over the radio rather than what is actually seen on the ground. This leads to the primary concept of vehicular surveillance: that only one surveillance vehicle is required to maintain visual command of the target vehicle at any given time. In fact, this is ideal since it limits the number of surveillance vehicles that are exposed to the target at any given time and provides the rest of the team increased flexibility in maneuvering.

The previous chapter concentrated on the stakeout and pickup, which initiate the follow phase of the operation. This discussion of vehicular surveillance will focus on tactics of the follow phase after the execution of a successful pickup.

INDIVIDUAL DUTIES AND RESPONSIBILITIES

Before discussing the tactics of the follow, a description of the specific duties of both the primary surveillance operators in a surveillance vehicle is necessary. To ensure optimal operational efficiency, each surveillance vehicle should have two operators— a *driver* and a *navigator*. Additional back seat operators can make valuable contributions but are not required.

The driver is the "eyes" of the surveillance vehicle. As will be discussed, the navigator has far too many duties to effectively maintain visual command of the target as well. For this reason, the driver must concentrate primarily on observing the target's movement and relaying these observations to the navigator. Additionally, the driver is responsible for driving safely and securely. The very nature of a surveillance operation dictates that operators drive aggressively, yet safely. There is no target that is worth the life of a team member. The surveillance driver must have the presence of mind to drive with technical proficiency while ensuring the safety of himself and his passengers.

In driving securely, the driver must be adept at the tactics of the follow and placement of the surveillance vehicle. This comprises an instinctive ability to maintain visual command of the target while blending with surrounding traffic to avoid drawing attention. The driver must be capable of reacting to the target's movements in a natural and tactically sound manner. He must also be capable of operating technical vehicle modifications as detailed in Chapter 3.

The tactics of a surveillance operation require that the driver be able to look ahead and anticipate possible hazards. To effectively maneuver through traffic the driver must read the flow of traffic ahead to ensure that his surveillance vehicle is not delayed while the target escapes. Particularly on fast routes such as highways, the driver should concentrate on all forward traffic rather than only the vehicles directly in front. This gives the driver early indicators as to which lane of travel will be the most effective. Additionally, by concentrating on the brake lights of vehicles further ahead, the driver can anticipate sudden stops more safely and effectively than waiting until the brake lights of the vehicle directly in front of him appear.

The passenger-side operator, or navigator, coordinates the activities of the surveillance vehicle. He must navigate (read the map), transmit the target's location and actions to the rest of the team, take notes, take photographs, and operate other technical equipment. With the driver relaying observations of the target, the navigator is free to read the map and transmit information to the team. Despite this, a technically sound navigator must possess the proficiency to navigate effectively with ample opportunity to observe the target as well. This frees the driver to maneuver in traffic as necessary and also ensures that the navigator does not draw undue attention to the surveillance vehicle from the target or surrounding traffic by constantly having his head bowed into his lap, reading the map. The navigator should also assist the driver in negotiating traffic by checking for oncoming traffic to the right at intersections and traffic on the highway when the surveillance vehicle is entering.

Map reading to the surveillance operator is much more difficult and complex than the standard interpretation would imply. This is a critical skill for the surveillance operator to master—in preparation for an operation and not while conducting one.

When in command of the target, the navigator must transmit timely and accurate directions of travel because the entire team is basing its actions on this information. The navigator must also be able to look ahead on the map to anticipate the target's actions.

When the surveillance vehicle is not in the position for visual command of the target, the driver simply drives and the navigator navigates. This may be a standard task for the driver, but it is a complex exercise for the navigator. When the surveillance vehicle has visual command of the target, the navigator is only concerned with the location of the target since his vehicle is in the same vicinity. When another surveillance vehicle is in command of the target, the navigator must track both the location of the target on the map as well as the location of his vehicle. At times the two may be on different pages in the map book. Whatever the case, the navigator must assess the location of his surveillance vehicle in relation to the target, analyze the terrain, and direct the driver to maneuver in a manner that best supports the overall team effort.

In many circumstances the driver is required to operate the surveillance vehicle without a navigator. This requires that the driver perform the duties of both the driver and navigator. The ultimate goal of any surveillance team is for all operators to possess the tactical and technical skills necessary to drive without a navigator at any time without losing effectiveness. The only relief of duties that a driver operating alone should expect is that, when he is in command of the target, another vehicle will take his notes based on radio transmissions.

SURVEILLANCE VEHICLE RESPONSIBILITIES AND DUTIIES

Command Vehicle

In order to have a surveillance follow, there must also be a surveillance vehicle with visual observation, or command, of the target. This surveillance vehicle is referred to as the *command vehicle*. The command vehicle is responsible for observing the target's activities and transmitting this information as it occurs. At this point, the command vehicle is literally in command of the surveillance operation because the entire team depends on that surveillance vehicle to transmit the appropriate information and to react effectively to the target.

Command Vehicle Calls

Transmissions that relay pertinent information about the activities of the target or other aspects that may have a direct impact on the operation in progress are referred to as *calls*. Any surveillance vehicle can make a call as necessary, but the command vehicle will always have priority over the radio network. The command vehicle will make calls regarding any observations of the target, which will assist the team in supporting the operation. During the follow, the command vehicle's most critical calls are made when the target turns onto another road, exits from the established road of travel, or stops and parks. These are particular situations in which the entire team reacts in a coordinated manner to the target's actions. The reactions of the team in such situations will be discussed in detail later in this and the next chapter. In addition to these calls, there are many other important observations which the command vehicle must relay to allow the team to position themselves appropriately.

Points of Reference

The standard call during the follow will include a point of reference that the team will recognize, either on the ground or on its maps, and a cardinal direction (north, south, east, west) of travel. The objective of such calls is to make it perfectly clear to the entire team where the target is and in which direction he is traveling. The best points of reference to use when informing the team of the target's location are those on the map. This ensures that the call benefits the entire team. Points that are not on the map benefit only those surveillance vehicles traveling along the same route of travel as the target. Standard points of reference include decision points, significant terrain features, man-made features, or landmarks. Decision points are locations where the target can possibly make a maneuver that will force the team to react and maneuver, such as a turn or an exit from the route of travel.

The most accurate points of reference are marked intersections because the team members can easily orient themselves on the map. The most basic use of these is to inform the team as the target continues straight through an intersection. By identifying specifically which intersection the target is passing, the road he is on, and his cardinal direction of travel, all members of the team are able to identify exactly where they are in relation to the target.

Points of reference are not limited to decision points. Any point of reference that appears on the map will assist the individual surveillance vehicles in maneuvering in accordance with the target's location. Such points include overpasses, railroad tracks, bus stops, parks, and monuments that are reflected on the map.

Recall that map books can be prepared by placing colored dots with corresponding numbers on points of reference that appear on the map. This practice allows the command vehicle to identify a point of reference by calling the numbered dot rather than specifying it by name. This facilitates radio brevity and enhanced security by not disclosing names and locations that can be identified if radio transmissions are intercepted.

Although of less overall benefit to the team, the use of points of reference that are not on the map can prove effective in many situations. Such points of reference are beneficial only to those surveillance vehicles traveling along the same route as the target and the command vehicle. These are particularly appropriate in rural areas where there are limited points of reference reflected on the map. They can include specified restaurants, stores, churches, construction sites, and unique signs. The use of such points is normally necessary on highway follows where the speed of travel in relation to the number of points reflected on the map is much faster than normal. The use of points of reference not on the map is generally more effective on the highways because during such follows the team is normally traveling along the same high-speed route as the target. Signs that indicate the number of miles to a specified city are particularly effective for use as points of reference.

An effective technique to employ when orienting a surveillance vehicle to a point of reference that is not on the map is to reset the odometer button. This technique is only effective when the surveillance vehicle employing it is following along the same route as the target and command vehicle. As the command vehicle notifies the team that the target has passed by a point of reference that is not on the map, the other team members along that route can reset their odometers. When their surveillance vehicle reaches the specified point of reference, they can determine how far behind they are in relation to the target by reading their odometer. This tactic can also be used for points that are on the map when it is difficult to judge distance from the map alone.

There is another odometer-reset technique that the command vehicle can employ to assist the other surveillance vehicles in orienting themselves in relation to the target. Once again, this technique is only effective when the surveillance vehicle employing it is on the same route of travel as the target and command vehicle. The command vehicle identifies a point of reference, such as a city-limit sign, and directs the team to reset their odometers when they reach that point. By doing this, the command vehicle can simply relay the mileage readings from its reset odometer to the other surveillance vehicles as the follow progresses. This provides the team specific information as to where they are in relation to the target. When this tactic is used in conjunction with a point that is reflected on the map, surveillance vehicles that are not on the same route can monitor the target's location by estimating distance on the map.

Indications of Intentions

An important category of calls for the command vehicle to report is that which identifies possible intentions of the target. The command vehicle should always be cognizant of the target's activities that may indicate what actions he intends to make. By relaying this information, the rest of the team is better able to maneuver in a manner to anticipate and react to the target. The most basic of these indications is when the target engages his turn signal. Although this is only a factor of seconds, even the shortest amount of time can be critical in a fast-moving and fluid surveillance operation.

Another less telling indication is the lane in which the target is traveling when on a multiple-lane road. Informing the team that the target is in the left lane indicates that the most likely turn to be made, if any, will be a left. This also indicates to the team that a right turn at that point is unlikely. Another indication is when the target slows, either slightly or significantly, at each intersection as though to read the street signs. This indicates that the target is approaching the street at which he will turn. On the highway, if the target travels in the left lane while approaching an exit, this is another indicator that he intends to continue straight on. Conversely, if the target slows his pace and approaches the exit while in the right lane, this may be an indication that he intends to exit.

It is small points like these that are incorporated into a comprehensive professional surveillance effort. As the reader progresses in the art of surveillance, the degree to which he will be able to observe surrounding traffic for indications of intentions will increase significantly. One will begin to realize how easy it is to anticipate the movements of another vehicle. The defensive driver attempts this every day—the surveillance operator applies this to his profession.

Travel Patterns of the Target

It is important for the command vehicle to report any significant characteristics of the target's travel patterns. These patterns will include, but are not limited to, speed, pace, and smoothness. This is important for various reasons. Most basically, such information allows team members to maneuver in accordance with the appropriate travel patterns and to be prepared when they assume command vehicle responsibilities.

Another more complex reason is that the target tends to alter his travel patterns when either preoccupied or traveling with a purpose. Years of surveillance experience have proven that the target will tend to act in an uncharacteristic manner when preparing to engage in illegal or operational activity. This shift in pattern may be intentional or not, depending on the target. Examples of such shifts in pattern are that the target may travel faster or more erratically, or he may travel slower and more deliberately. Whatever the case, if the surveillance team has examined the target's travel patterns sufficiently, any alteration should become readily apparent. The most significant of these alterations is that the target becomes more observant and conscious of his surroundings, indicating possible surveillance detection. Evasive maneuvers are of course indicative of antisurveillance.

A very important aspect of the target's travel activity, which the command vehicle should call as appropriate, is speed. The command vehicle simply gauges the target's speed by pacing itself at a sufficient distance behind the target. Pacing does not imply that the command vehicle mirrors the movements of the target. It takes little time and distance to gauge the speed of the target and is only done when it is unobservable or would appear natural to the target. Speed calls allow the team to gauge its own speed while maneuvering in the follow. Among other aspects, these calls prevent the following surveillance vehicles from pushing too far up or falling too far behind. Regular speed calls also assist the team in estimating the target's speed when conducting a lost-command drill, which will be discussed in the next chapter.

Backing Vehicle Duties and Responsibilities

The only surveillance vehicle other than the command vehicle with designated responsibilities during a given sequence of the follow is the *backing vehicle*. The backing vehicle is the next surveillance vehicle in sequence behind the command vehicle that is in position to take command of the target at any time. This is not to say that the next surveillance vehicle behind the command vehicle is necessarily in position to be considered a backing vehicle. A surveillance vehicle is not backing until it is in a position to comfortably assume command of the target when directed to do so by the command vehicle.

During the follow it is appropriate for the backing vehicle to acknowledge the calls of the command vehicle. This continuously reinforces to the command vehicle that it has a backing vehicle. This is important because the command vehicle never knows when a situation may arise that requires it to pass command of the target to the backing vehicle. Knowing that it has a backing vehicle gives the command vehicle more flexibility in reacting to unexpected actions by the target.

As stated previously, the only two vehicles with specific duties during a given portion of the follow are the command and backing vehicles. The command and backing vehicle positions will rotate among all of the team's vehicles as the follow develops and circumstances dictate. The remaining vehicles on the team, other than the command and backing vehicles, have the flexibility to maneuver as they deem best to support the team effort.

SURVEILLANCE VEHICLE POSITIONING AND ACTIONS

During a straight follow, in which most of the surveillance vehicles are traveling along the same route as the target, there are some general principles that will assist the team in maneuvering without drawing the target's attention. These principles are directly related to the concept of blending with the surrounding traffic to appear natural. They apply to all surveillance vehicles, to include the command and backing vehicles.

Following Distance

The command vehicle will maintain a following distance that allows it to maintain visual command of the target. It is preferable that there be at least one vehicle between the command vehicle and the target to provide cover, but this is not always possible. Whatever the case, the command vehicle should maintain a pace that is natural in relation to the route and surrounding traffic. The command vehicle may tend to gain a sense of security by maintaining a large amount of distance between itself and the target. In doing this, the surveillance vehicle may slow down unnaturally to fall farther back, perhaps even to the point of slowing down other traffic and making this unnatural action even more visible to the target.

In many cases, if the command vehicle is obstructed by a traffic obstacle, there will be no other surveillance vehicle in position to maneuver around the obstacle and assume command of the target. For this reason, the command vehicle must account for traffic obstacles such as traffic lights and traffic density when distancing itself from the target. Significant traffic obstacles will normally dictate that the command vehicle maintain a decreased following distance.

The backing vehicle's following distance will be dictated by what is necessary to support the command vehicle and complete its duties, as discussed previously. Generally, the backing vehicle will maintain a distance that allows it to observe the command vehicle while remaining out of the target's sight. In determining the appropriate following distance, the backing vehicle must read ahead to anticipate traffic obstacles that may obstruct it from establishing the command position. In many situations, the terrain and traffic will dictate that the backing vehicle also maintain visual observation of the target. This is appropriate if there is sufficient cover for the backing vehicle, but ideally only one surveillance vehicle will be exposed to the target at any given time. The backing vehicle may also select to close its following distance when the target is approaching a major traffic option such as a highway. Such hazards may dictate that the backing vehicle be in position to establish immediate command of the target if necessary.

Surveillance vehicles in the follow do not adhere to any

standard rules for distance between each other. Once again, the only guideline is that they should maneuver in a manner that is natural and blends with the surrounding traffic. Ideally, a surveillance vehicle will maintain visual observation of the next surveillance vehicle in front of it, just as the backing vehicle does with the command vehicle. The only rule that the remaining surveillance vehicles must follow is that they should not pass the backing or command vehicles on the same road of travel, for obvious reasons.

The remaining surveillance vehicles should not be in file directly behind the backing vehicle when following on the same road. This raises the possibility of exposing three or more surveillance vehicles to the target at one time. Additionally, the closer the surveillance vehicles push in behind the backing vehicle, the less flexibility the team has in reacting to the target. For example, if the team is following closely and the target suddenly pulls over and parks, the entire team has the same limited option to pull off before it is forced past the target's location. This results in an unnecessary number of surveillance vehicles being exposed to the target. This also makes it difficult for the team to set up a quick and effective surveillance box to reestablish command of the target.

This point once again highlights the importance of a radio communications system. By relying on the calls of the command vehicle, the remaining surveillance vehicles have the flexibility to establish a secure following distance without relying on observations of the target or other surveillance vehicles to guide them.

General Tactics of the Follow

It is critical to the success of a vehicular surveillance that all the operators be familiar with the other surveillance vehicles on the team. This is necessary because it allows the team to position itself in relation to the other surveillance vehicles and to avoid passing other surveillance vehicles and unnecessarily exposing itself to the target.

One technique that can be used when one surveillance vehicle is unsure whether a vehicle ahead of it is a team member or not is the "tap-red" method. The trailing surveillance vehicle will ask, over the radio, for the surveillance vehicle in question to "tap red."

The driver of that surveillance vehicle will, in turn, tap lightly on the brake pedal as the navigator transmits "tapping red." A light tap will engage the brake light without engaging the brakes.

If the trailing surveillance vehicle sees the brake lights of the other surveillance vehicle, it will transmit "red seen," indicating that it is positioned behind the now identified surveillance vehicle. If no brake lights are seen, the requesting surveillance vehicle will transmit "nothing seen," indicating to the other surveillance vehicle that it is not positioned behind him. At this point the requesting surveillance vehicle will be assured that the vehicle in question is not a team member and is free to move ahead without risk of passing a fellow surveillance vehicle. This tactic is invaluable during night surveillance operations.

During the follow, surveillance vehicles should avoid mirroring the actions of the target. Mirroring refers to duplicating the exact maneuver of the target. A very simple form of surveillance detection is for the target to observe traffic in his rear-view mirror to determine if any of the vehicles behind him are reacting to his actions. Detection tactics such as altering pace and changing lanes frequently may be used to this end. Obviously, the command vehicle is most vulnerable to detection and must be particularly sure not to mirror. One method that the team will use to avoid mirroring the target is to exchange command of the target when he makes a turn. This method will be discussed in detail in the next section.

The most common mirroring error is to change lanes as the target does. This should be avoided unless absolutely necessary because it can be easily observed by the target through his rear-view mirror. Another form of mirroring is for a surveillance vehicle to maintain a steady pace with the target. It can become very obvious to the target when a vehicle is speeding up and slowing as he does. The command vehicle particularly should avoid this error. If necessary, it should pass the target to maintain a natural appearance, but this should be avoided when possible because it gives the target a good look at the surveillance vehicle.

Even if the command vehicle is forced to pass, it can remain in command through the use of its rear-view mirror. When doing this the command vehicle should ensure that there is sufficient distance between it and the target, and once again it should avoid mirroring while in front of the target.

Recall how the brake light kill switch can be used to discreetly decrease speed under these circumstances. When this occurs, the command vehicle must inform the team that it is in command of the target from in front—primarily to inform the backing vehicle that there is no surveillance vehicle between him and the target. This ensures that the backing vehicle does not bear down unnaturally on the target.

When following the target vehicle, the command vehicle should appear absolutely natural. This is particularly the case when following closely in heavy traffic or when stopped at a traffic light. The navigator of the command vehicle cannot stop transmitting information in these situations. To avoid appearing suspicious, the navigator should turn his head toward the driver when transmitting information to the team. If the target is observing in his rear-view mirror, this will appear as though the occupants of the surveillance vehicle are having a normal conversation.

COMMAND AND BACKING
VEHICLE EXCHANGE OF COMMAND

As discussed previously, the most critical calls the command vehicle will make are when the target turns onto another road, exits from the road of travel, or stops and parks. These are situations that cause the team to react. They also cause the command vehicle to determine whether or not it will turn or stop with the target. Only in situations where there is exceptional cover will the command vehicle pull over and stop when the target does. This is a risky maneuver because it is at such times that the target is very conscious of his surroundings. It is also unnecessary with other surveillance vehicles in the follow. The tactics of the surveillance box, which are established when the target stops, will be discussed in the next chapter.

When the target makes a turn, immediate and automatic coordination must be executed between the command and backing vehicles. At the instant the command vehicle observes the target making the turn, the navigator must determine, as he is transmitting the information, whether his vehicle will maintain command. Generally, if the command vehicle has a backing vehicle and team integrity is good, he will turn over command to the backing vehicle. Command is normally exchanged when the target makes a turn as a standard security precaution, due to the fact that a target practicing surveillance detection will watch to see if the vehicles behind him take the same turn.

In some circumstances, traffic flow and cover are adequate for the command vehicle to maintain command by taking the turn behind the target. For example, if the turn the target takes follows the general flow of traffic, it is appropriate for the command vehicle to blend with the surrounding traffic and take that turn as well.

This decision is a judgment call by the navigator of the command vehicle. Whatever the decision, it is important to note that taking more than one turn with the target can significantly risk the security of the operation.

When the command vehicle determines that it is necessary to exchange command after the target turns, the coordination must be fluid and natural. Directly after the command vehicle transmits the appropriate information regarding the turn, that surveillance vehicle will also transmit that he is "off." This indicates to the backing vehicle that the command vehicle has continued straight at the intersection. With this, the backing vehicle will acknowledge the call and take the turn to maneuver for command of the target.

Immediately upon establishing command, that surveillance vehicle will transmit the status of the target and inform the team that it is the command vehicle. As this occurs, another appropriate surveillance vehicle will maneuver to establish the backing position. When a backing vehicle is established, that surveillance vehicle will inform the team of such as the follow continues. The remaining surveillance vehicles will maneuver to support the follow as they determine best. Figure 10 depicts the exchange of command between command vehicle Alpha and backing vehicle Bravo in reaction to a turn by the target.

Surveillance vehicles are not restricted to exchanging command only in reaction to a turn by the target. At any time the navigator of the command vehicle judges that it is necessary to relinquish command of the target to the backing vehicle, this can be done with minor coordination. The command vehicle will normally make the decision based on its amount of time in com-

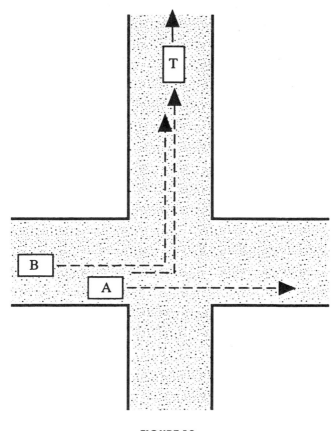

FIGURE 10

mand and the degree to which it may have been exposed to the target. Remember that in a coordinated surveillance with multiple surveillance vehicles, there is rarely justification for exposing one surveillance vehicle to a degree that might risk the security of the operation.

When the command vehicle needs to exchange command, it will notify the backing vehicle to execute an exchange at a specified intersection or location. The backing vehicle will acknowledge that it is in position for the exchange, and the coordination is complete. Normally, intersections are the most appropriate locations for exchanges because the command vehicle can turn off naturally. If the target turns at the specified exchange point, the command vehicle will continue straight, and the backing

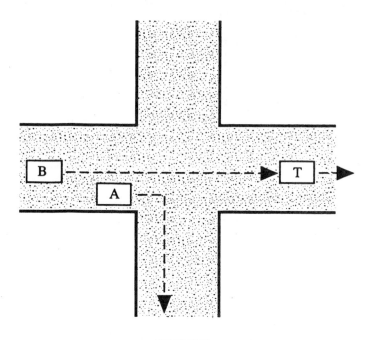

FIGURE 11

vehicle will follow the target through the turn to assume command (identical to Figure 10). Conversely, if the target continues straight, the command vehicle will turn at that location, and the backing vehicle will continue straight to assume command of the target. Figure 11 depicts this exchange of command between command vehicle Alpha and backing vehicle Bravo.

When an exchange is executed on a two-way road, the command vehicle should make every effort to turn right as the exchange is executed. This ensures that oncoming traffic does not impede the command vehicle's ability to turn left, thus obstructing the backing vehicle from maneuvering forward to assume command of the target. Exchanges at intersections with traffic lights should be avoided when possible. Such intersections pose the possibility of the backing vehicle being stopped by the light after the command vehicle has turned off.

There is one variation of this maneuver that the command vehicle can execute when there is no backing vehicle. This involves the command vehicle traveling straight through an intersection after the target turns. After the surveillance vehicle

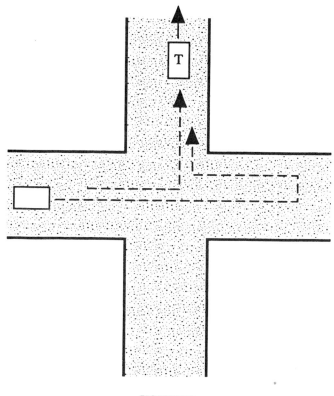

FIGURE 12

clears the intersection, it will execute a U-turn back to the intersection and turn in the direction of the target (see Figure 12).

This maneuver breaks the profile of the surveillance vehicle turning directly behind the target and also provides the surveillance vehicle some distance from the target. Although this technique can be effective in maintaining command of the target, it is a very risky maneuver from both the surveillance detection and countersurveillance standpoint.

ADVANCED VEHICULAR SURVEILLANCE

The previous chapter comprised an introduction to the minimum degree of tactical knowledge necessary to conduct a vehicular surveillance. With an understanding of these basics, the reader is capable of conducting a standard operation. Many of these previously discussed tactics can be employed in a single-vehicle surveillance. This chapter, however, addresses the comprehensive team tactical applications that are indicative of those employed by the surveillance team.

THE FLOATING BOX

Chapter 5 discussed the employment of a stakeout box to initiate command of the target. Recall how surveillance vehicles position themselves in a manner to cover all the target's possible routes of travel. The same principle of dispersing surveillance vehicles to cover multiple routes of travel is employed in vehicular surveillance through the floating box. The primary conceptual difference between the *floating box* and the *static box* is that with the floating box, the team will rarely attempt to position a surveillance vehicle ahead of the target on an established route of travel. The reason for this is that it is difficult for a forward surveillance vehicle to maintain a pace that supports the effort while ensuring that it remains out of the target's view. A surveillance vehicle can be much more effectively positioned elsewhere in the floating box.

As with many team tactics of vehicular surveillance, the floating box is possible primarily through reliance on effective communications. In fact, since the floating box relies on the use of parallel roads, some of the surveillance vehicles involved will be on separate streets from that of the target and the command vehicle. Although ours is not a perfect world, with perfectly straight roads and perfectly square blocks, this concept is applicable in many situations.

After the command and backing vehicles have been established, the remaining surveillance vehicles will begin to assess their positions in relation to the target. By analyzing their maps, the navigators will determine how their surveillance vehicle can best support the team. If the terrain is suitable for a floating box, the appropriate surveillance vehicles will notify the team and maneuver to paralleling roads. In many situations it will be difficult to maneuver directly from a straight follow to a floating box. As will be displayed in figures, after the target makes a turn, the team can transition from a straight follow to a floating box with relative ease.

Figure 13 depicts the surveillance team in a straight follow with surveillance vehicle Alpha in command. As the target turns right at the intersection, Alpha continues straight and surveillance vehicle Delta turns behind the target to assume command. Surveillance vehicle Echo, being in the best position to do so, maneuvers behind Delta to assume the backing position. Surveillance vehicle Charlie also continues to maneuver along the same route to reinforce the follow. At this point surveillance vehicles Alpha and Golf are in position to establish the initial floating box.

Figure 14 depicts how Alpha and Golf maneuver to establish the floating box. Alpha informs the team that it is maneuvering to the left parallel and continues to the next intersection. Alpha then turns right and parallels the rest of the team to the north. Golf informs the team that it is maneuvering to the right parallel.

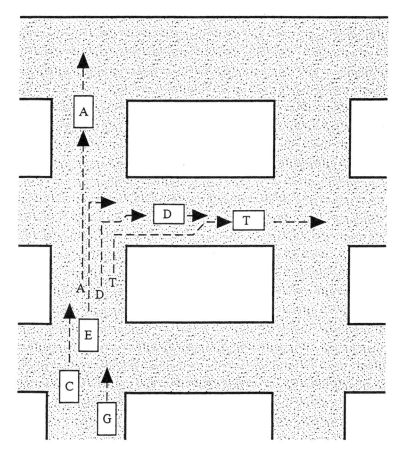

FIGURE 13

Golf then turns right at the intersection prior to the intersection at which the target turned and parallels the team to the south. As command vehicle Delta calls the target through the next intersection, surveillance vehicles Alpha and Golf continue straight through the corresponding intersections along their routes, remaining on the north and south parallels respectively. Surveillance vehicle Charlie remains far enough behind the backing vehicle to be able to pull off the road undetected in the event that the target executes an unexpected U-turn. Notice that surveillance vehicles Alpha and Golf are in position to stop and establish box positions if the target turns right or left at any

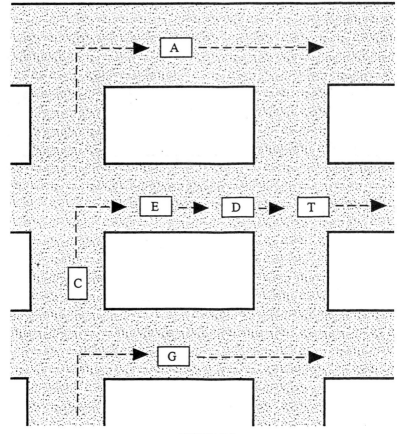

FIGURE 14

of the intersections along the road. At this point surveillance vehicles Charlie, Alpha, and Golf constitute the floating box.

Continuing from the previous figure, Figure 15 depicts how the floating box provides an added dimension of effectiveness to the surveillance operation. After traveling straight for some distance, the target takes another right turn and travels south. Surveillance vehicle Delta informs the team of the turn and continues straight to exchange command with Echo. Delta continues to the next intersection to turn right and travel south along the left parallel. Echo, however, is obstructed by traffic and is temporarily unable to turn right behind the target. Surveillance vehi-

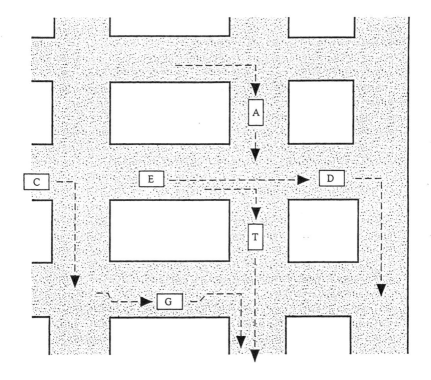

FIGURE 15

cle Golf pulls over along its parallel route prior to the next intersection to establish a control box position. Surveillance vehicle
Alpha continues to the intersection along its parallel route and
turns right to travel south on the same route as the target.

Surveillance vehicle Charlie, which was holding back to cover
the rear of the box, is in position to turn right at the intersection
prior to the one at which the target turned and traveled south on
the right parallel. As the target passes the intersection at which
Golf is positioned to control, Golf commits the target by informing the team, turns right, and travels south to establish command
of the target. Alpha continues to maneuver south to establish a

backing position. When surveillance vehicle Echo is clear to turn, it will turn right and travel south to reinforce the follow. At this point, the follow with the floating box has been reestablished, with Delta and Charlie on the right and left (east and west) parallels, respectively, and Echo covering the rear of the box.

In the previous example, had Echo been able to turn right and establish command of the target, only surveillance vehicle Golf's actions would have been different. Golf would have remained in its control box position until after the target, surveillance vehicle Echo, and perhaps even Alpha had passed by before pulling out and turning right to join the follow.

SURVEILLANCE BOX

In Chapter 5, the principles of the stakeout box were discussed. Recall that the stakeout box is employed to establish initial command of the target. A box established directly after the target comes to a stop during the course of a surveillance follow shares most of the same tactics as those introduced with stakeouts. The primary difference is that a box established subsequent to a follow will normally have some degree of command over the target. In such circumstances, command will be exercised by static observation of the target or a trigger surveillance vehicle on the target vehicle and a box that covers all the possible routes away from the point of the stop.

Anytime the target stops, excluding normal traffic stops, a surveillance box will be placed around the target to cover all possible routes of travel from the location of the stop. Unlike the stakeout, when boxing under these circumstances, the team will usually have no information from which to select their box positions other than the location of the target, maps, and immediate observations.

As with all aspects of a professional surveillance effort, the application of an effective box is the result of a tactically proficient team operating with a unity of effort. This effort depends on the speed, initiative, and judgment of the individual surveillance vehicles. When establishing the box, the team can never be sure how long the target will remain stopped. If the target begins to maneuver before the box is established, he may depart undetected.

A successful box begins with a timely and accurate call from the command vehicle, indicating that the target has stopped and providing its exact location. By identifying the exact location of the stop, the team members can maneuver to establish the box without filing past the target and exposing themselves unnecessarily. The location of the stop must be given in terms that can be identified on the map and not by features that must be observed on the ground. This allows the team to determine where to maneuver by analyzing the map rather than actually observing the target's location.

Maps with alphanumeric grid designators can be used to pinpoint the target's location. Grids are divided by a factor of 10, either by visual estimate or by the use of a transparent protractor for exact positioning. The target vehicle's location will be given by an alphabetic grid and numeric grid reading. Navigators will normally make a visual grid estimate rather than using a protractor because of time constraints.

The first priority in establishing the box is to establish a static observation of the target or a trigger surveillance vehicle on the target vehicle. If the target exits his vehicle and goes to ground, the team must transition to a foot surveillance for the follow to continue. Chapter 10 addresses this transition in detail.

A *surveillance vehicle with static observation of the target* is one that observes the target who is still in his vehicle or standing close by. A *trigger surveillance vehicle* is one that can observe the target vehicle when the target has exited and departed. Either a static observation or a trigger surveillance vehicle gives the team a degree of command because both inform the team when the target vehicle begins to move. For the purposes of this discussion, a trigger surveillance vehicle will be assumed since this is most commonly the case.

When the target stops, the command vehicle will travel past and maneuver to establish a box position. Due to security reasons, the command vehicle should not be the one that establishes the trigger position. This is one of the points at which the target will be most observant of his surroundings. A vehicle that follows in sight of the target and then parks in the same vicinity presents an unnecessary risk, provided that there is another surveillance vehicle in the area to establish a trigger. Usually, the backing vehicle will be the one that maneuvers to establish the trigger. This is not a hard-and-fast rule, but, once again, it is best to minimize the number of surveillance vehicles that pass by the parked target.

Once a trigger has been established, the remaining surveillance vehicles will maneuver to establish the box, using the same principles discussed in the stakeout examples. Generally, priority of positioning in the box will be determined by assessing the target's most likely routes of departure, based on the location where he is parked. Navigators will determine which route their surveillance vehicle will box and direct their drivers to that location. As this is initiated, the navigator will inform the rest of the team as to the route that his surveillance vehicle intends to box. This will ensure that duplication of effort and wasted time are minimized.

During this process, the team is constantly analyzing possible routes by which the target may depart to ensure that there are no holes in the box. Once a given surveillance vehicle reaches its box position, it will inform the team of such. The box is established when all possible routes of departure are covered by surveillance vehicles. Any remaining surveillance vehicles will establish reinforcing box positions based on prioritization of the most likely routes of departure, traffic obstacles, and traffic hazards.

Figure 16 depicts a standard execution of the box after the target stops. Surveillance vehicles Alpha, Bravo, Charlie, Delta, and Echo are involved in a straight follow. As command vehicle Alpha calls the target entering a parking lot, it continues straight to establish a box position. Surveillance vehicle Bravo, the backing vehicle, maneuvers to establish a trigger position. The remaining surveillance vehicles maneuver to their box positions by the use of routes that allow them to avoid passing by the target's location.

Figure 17 depicts the box after it is established. Bravo is established as the trigger. The arrows depict the control assignments of the remaining surveillance vehicles.

When there are not enough surveillance vehicles to cover all the target's possible routes of travel, adjustments must be made. Although a trigger surveillance vehicle is ideal, it should not be employed at the expense of leaving a route of departure uncovered. A box is still effective without a trigger if all routes of travel are covered. If surveillance vehicles are limited or there are simply too many routes to be covered, further adjustments must be

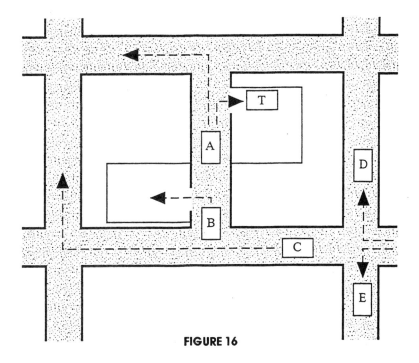

FIGURE 16

made. The least desirable is to leave routes uncovered. When this is necessary, the selection of the route(s) to remain uncovered will be based on a prioritization of the least likely routes of departure. Another option is to collapse the box in closer to the target in an effort to decrease the possible routes of departure. This option decreases the degree of security by bringing additional surveillance vehicles closer to the target's location.

When the target vehicle begins to depart, the team will execute a pickup and follow as the box is broken, similar to those of the stakeout pickup and follow.

TEAM REACTION TO A U-TURN

When the target makes a U-turn during the vehicular follow, the team must react immediately to minimize exposure and to maximize the possibility of continuing the follow. As the command vehicle informs the team that the target has executed a U-

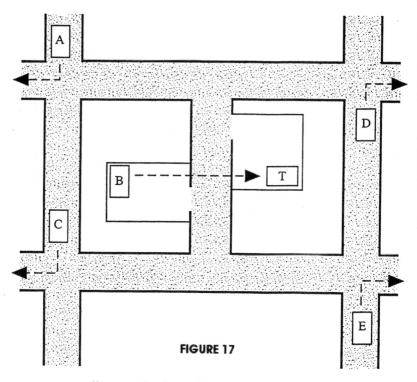

FIGURE 17

turn, surveillance vehicles will immediately attempt to pull off the road, ideally onto adjacent roads. This should not be done in an unnatural manner, which can be observed by the target.

In turning onto adjacent roads, the surveillance vehicles should attempt to turn off to the left. This will facilitate establishing a more effective control position by allowing them to make a right turn onto the main road when entering to establish command of the target vehicle as it passes back by. Additionally, roads the target can turn onto after executing the U-turn must be immediately boxed by surveillance vehicles. This is important because the most common reason for a coincidental U-turn is that the target has missed a turn and must backtrack to recover.

Unless the team reacts immediately to box the area of the U-turn, the target's mistake may become an unintentional, yet effective, antisurveillance maneuver. A hard or overt target may also execute a U-turn as a deliberate antisurveillance or surveillance detection maneuver.

Figure 18 depicts the team's reaction to an unexpected U-turn

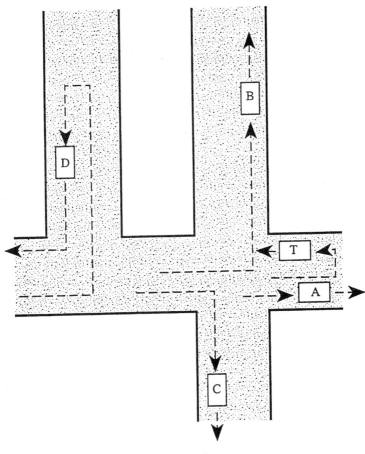

FIGURE 18

by the target. Surveillance vehicle Alpha informs the team of the turn while surveillance vehicles Bravo, Charlie, and Delta immediately maneuver to establish a hasty box to cover the target's possible routes of travel. The arrow in front of each of the surveillance vehicles depicts their control intentions.

THE LOST-COMMAND DRILL

During the course of the follow, the team may lose command of the target. This can occur for several reasons, such as bends in the road, poor visibility, traffic obstacles, bad luck, poor execution, or antisurveillance conducted by the target. It may also occur because the command vehicle has no backing vehicle to exchange command with and must break off because of security reasons. In the event of lost command, there are certain tactics that the team must execute to maximize the possibility of regaining command. This is done through the *lost-command drill*, which is a systematic sequence of maneuvers executed to regain command of the target.

When the command vehicle initially loses command of the target, it will immediately inform the team that the target is "temporarily (temp) unsighted." This indicates to the team that the command vehicle has lost visual command of the target, but it has not passed an option that the target may have taken undetected. The team will understand it is probable that the target is still traveling along the same route, only ahead and out of sight of the command vehicle.

As the command vehicle moves ahead and attempts to reestablish command of the target, the remaining surveillance vehicles will close their following distance in anticipation of the worst. If the team is fortunate enough to have surveillance vehicles on paralleling routes, those surveillance vehicles will continue forward to positions that cover paralleling options. When the command vehicle reestablishes command of the target, the team will be informed and the follow will continue. Understand that the "temp unsighted" call is a precautionary measure to be used freely, whenever necessary. In many follows, particularly on winding roads, the "temp unsighted" call will be used frequently. Again, in most cases it will simply be a precautionary call to prepare the team for a possible lost command.

If the target has been called "temp unsighted" and remains unsighted when the command vehicle approaches or reaches an option the target could have taken, the command vehicle will then inform the team that the target is "unsighted." At this point, the team will immediately begin to execute a lost-command drill. This is necessary because, even though the target may have continued straight at the option, there is also a possibility that the target turned off.

It is always to the team's advantage to have surveillance vehicles previously traveling on parallel routes when the lost-command drill is initiated. Recall from the discussion of the floating box that surveillance vehicles on parallel routes are in position to immediately establish control positions at paralleling options when the target takes a turn. This same concept applies in the lost-command drill when there is a possibility that the target turned at an option. For the purposes of this discussion, however, the lost-command drill will be explained under the scenario that all the surveillance vehicles are traveling along the same route.

As the lost-command drill is initiated, the (formerly) command vehicle will take the most logical route that the target would have taken at that option. This route will normally be straight at the option. An example of when the (formerly) command vehicle would take a route other than straight is when one of the routes from the option leads to a traffic hazard, such as a highway. As that surveillance vehicle begins to check for the target along the initial route, it will inform the team of its intentions. It is important that each surveillance vehicle inform the team of its actions as the lost-command drill progresses. This ensures that there is no duplication of effort, such as two surveillance vehicles checking along the same route while leaving another route unchecked.

The second surveillance vehicle to the location of lost command will check along the second most logical route of travel. As the third surveillance vehicle reaches the location of lost command it will take the third most logical route of travel. This will continue until all possible routes are being checked or there are no surveillance vehicles remaining to check additional routes. When all possible routes are being checked, any remaining surveillance vehicles will maneuver to reinforce along a route that is already being checked. This will be done in the same order of priority as designated by the initial checking surveillance vehicles.

Figure 19 illustrates the lost-command drill executed at a standard X intersection. As command vehicle Alpha reaches the intersection and informs the team that the target is unsighted, it checks the most logical route that the target would have taken— in this case straight. As surveillance vehicle Bravo reaches the intersection it takes the next most logical route—in this case to the right. As surveillance vehicle Charlie reaches the intersection it takes the only remaining route to the left. When surveillance vehicle Delta reaches the intersection it will reinforce Alpha along the straight route. Surveillance vehicle Echo will in turn reinforce Bravo to the right, and, finally, Golf will reinforce Charlie to the left. When one of the surveillance vehicles reestablishes command of the target it will inform the team, and the follow will continue.

Obviously, this drill significantly degrades team integrity. When command is reestablished, the surveillance vehicles on the other routes will maneuver to recover as quickly as possible. Once a lost-command drill has been initiated, the surveillance vehicles have no other option but to check along the route to which they are committed. To attempt to check additional auxiliary roads along the route will diminish their ability to locate the target along the primary route they are checking. Each surveillance vehicle should, however, attempt to make visual checks of each road it passes. In doing so, it is most effective for the drivers to look down the roads to the right as they travel straight and for the navigators to look to the left. This is the easiest and safest way to check side streets and still maintain forward observation. They should also make every effort to visually check areas such as parking lots and service stations.

In situations when there is more than one surveillance vehicle checking along the same route, a second surveillance vehicle along that route may select to check another road off that route. This is done if another major option the target may have taken is reached. If this is done, it will never be the first surveillance vehicle checking along the route because it is the one in the best position to catch the target along the initial route. The disadvantage in a surveillance vehicle checking another route is that it further degrades team integrity. When a surveillance vehicle reestablishes command of the target during the lost-command drill, it is obviously ideal to have another surveillance vehicle reinforcing close behind.

In the lost-command drill, surveillance vehicles will use the *time-distance method* to determine how far out they continue to check for the target. A time-distance determination is made when a surveillance vehicle checking along a route determines the point at which it would have reestablished command of the target had the target been traveling along

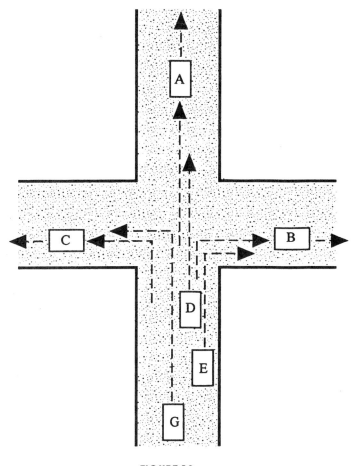

FIGURE 19

that route. This is done through either a logical deduction or mathematical calculations based on the target's previously identified rate of speed, the speed at which the surveillance vehicle has been checking, and the distance along the route that has been checked.

The time-distance formula is an equation used to determine how far and at what rate of speed the surveillance vehicle must travel to catch the target. In virtually all cases, this will be based on an educated estimate rather than actually figuring the equation while conducting a lost-command drill. Actual calculations can be effective in some situations, however, particularly when conducting a lost-command drill on the highway. The time-distance formula is as follows:

$$Distance = Speed \times Time$$
or
$$Time = Distance/Speed$$
or
$$Speed = Distance/Time$$

To use this formula, the surveillance vehicle must have an estimated speed at which the target is traveling. If the follow or the operation has been ongoing, the team should have a good idea of the average speed at which the target travels on different types of roads. The surveillance vehicle must also keep track of how far it is from the location of lost command. This is most easily done by resetting the odometer immediately after the target is called unsighted. The time factor for the time-distance formula is one hour = 1. In order to get the factor for times less than one hour, a factor of 60 must be divided into the number of minutes. Some standard time factors are as follows:

$$15 \text{ min. } (15/60) = .25$$
$$10 \text{ min. } (10/60) = .17$$
$$5 \text{ min. } (5/60) = .08$$
$$3 \text{ min. } (3/60) = .05$$

For example, the target has been unsighted for one minute at the time that a surveillance vehicle reaches the location of unsighted to begin checking a possible route of travel. The target had been traveling at an average speed of 30 miles per hour (MPH). By use of the equation, the surveillance vehicle can calculate that the target is one-half mile ahead. This is figured as follows:

$$Distance = Speed \times Time$$
$$Distance = 30 \times 60/1$$
$$Distance = 30 \times .02$$
$$30 \times .02 = Distance \text{ of } .5 \ (1/2 \text{ mile})$$

The surveillance vehicle, now having a better idea of how much distance it must make up, will obviously have to travel at a speed greater than 30 MPH—but of course it did not need the formula to deduce this. After checking for three minutes at 40 MPH the surveillance vehicle can see from his odometer that it has traveled two miles. By the equation this is as follows:

$$\text{Distance} = \text{Speed} \times \text{Time}$$
$$2 = 40 \times 3/60$$
$$2 = 40 \times .05$$

The surveillance vehicle then figures the equation for the target. Recall that the target had been unsighted for one minute prior to the surveillance vehicle reaching the location of unsighted. For this reason the time factor for the target will be four minutes. The equation for the target is as follows:

$$\text{Distance} = \text{Speed} \times \text{Time}$$
$$\text{Distance} = 30 \times 4/60$$
$$\text{Distance} = 30 \times .07$$
$$30 \times .07 = \text{Distance of 2 miles}$$

Therefore, based on the time/distance formula, if the target had taken that route, the surveillance vehicle would have reestablished command at that point. The surveillance vehicle can deduce that the target did not travel along that route from the point of lost command or that it turned off prior to that point.

Another example of when this formula can be used is one in which a surveillance vehicle begins to check for the target along a certain route. Looking ahead on the map, the surveillance vehicle can see that there is a major road option four miles ahead. Given this situation, the surveillance vehicle realizes that it must reestablish command of the target prior to that option, or else the possibility of finding the target is greatly diminished. To this end, the surveillance vehicle will figure the rate of speed that it must travel to reestablish command prior to that option. In this example the surveillance vehicle reaches the location of lost command one minute after the target was last sighted. The target was traveling at an average speed of 35 miles per hour. The equation for the target is as follows:

$$Distance = Speed \times Time$$
or
$$Time = Distance/Speed$$
$$Time = 4/35$$
$$.11 = 4/35$$

The time is .11 of an hour. The time of .11 is converted into minutes by multiplying it by 60.

$$60/.11 = 6.6$$

By this, the surveillance vehicle determines that the target will reach the option in approximately 6.6 minutes from the time of unsighted. For the surveillance vehicle to determine how fast it must travel to catch the target prior to the option, it must first figure the correct time factor. Recall that the surveillance vehicle reached the location of lost command one minute behind the target. This means that the surveillance vehicle has one minute less time to reach the option than does the target. This additional minute must be subtracted from the target's time to figure how fast the surveillance vehicle must travel. The adjusted time factor for the surveillance vehicle is 5.6. This number is reconverted by dividing it by a factor of 60.

$$Time = 5.6/60$$

The speed is then figured as follows:

$$Distance = Speed \times Time$$
or
$$Speed = Distance/Time$$
$$Speed = 4/.09$$
$$4/.09 = Speed \ of \ 44.44 \ MPH$$

This means that the vehicle should travel at a speed of at least

45 MPH in order to catch the target, if the target is in fact traveling along that route at a speed of 35 MPH or less.

The two previous examples represent common applications of the time-distance formula. Navigators must have immediate access to a calculator for fast and precise use of the formula. Exact calculations can be made in a matter of seconds, given a sound understanding of the formula and its many applications. As demonstrated, there are a number of uses for which the formula can be manipulated to satisfy situation-specific requirements.

The time-distance formula is a tool for situations in which exact calculations are desired. In most cases, however, time-distance determinations will be based on subjective judgments. Whether using the formula or subjective judgment when conducting a lost-command drill, a surveillance vehicle will check a route until it determines that, based on time-distance, the target could not have continued along that same route. Regardless of time-distance, a surveillance vehicle will normally only check a route as long as it remains in communications range. When radio communications become static filled and barely readable, the surveillance vehicle will normally terminate its checking drill along the route to avoid losing radio contact with the team. Telephones in the team's vehicles will allow a surveillance vehicle to check further if necessary.

When the target is located during a lost-command drill, team integrity is normally poor. With surveillance vehicles checking in opposite directions, it is possible that when a surveillance vehicle reestablishes command of the target there may be surveillance vehicles out of the communications range of the command vehicle. In such cases it is necessary for surveillance vehicles that are in range to relay information from the command vehicle to those out of range.

This practice is particularly applicable during the lost-command drill, but may be necessary during other portions of the follow. For example, if a surveillance vehicle stops for fuel during a highway follow, it is likely that the vehicle will be out of communications range with the command vehicle when it reenters the follow. In this case, the surveillance vehicle will require a relay of the command vehicle's calls from an intermediate surveillance vehicle.

After a surveillance vehicle has stopped checking along its

route for time-distance or communications reasons, it will inform the team of the negative results and begin to retrace its route back to the location of lost command. At this point, it is not necessary for the surveillance vehicle to remain strictly on the same route that it checked when working its way back. On the way back, the surveillance vehicle has the option to more thoroughly check areas that it passed where the target may have stopped. Such areas may consist of shopping centers or malls in the vicinity of the route. Previously developed information regarding the target may assist in these efforts. For example, if the target is known to frequent museums and there is one in the area, this would be a worthwhile location to check when returning.

As surveillance vehicles complete retracing their routes back to the location of lost command, they will begin to establish a stakeout box around the specific option of lost command in anticipation that the target may return through that location. The first surveillance vehicle to the location will establish a commit position at the specific option. The other surveillance vehicles will in turn establish appropriate box positions.

In some situations, such as lost command in residential areas, the team may choose to leave a surveillance vehicle at the option of lost command as the lost-command drill is initiated. During the course of the lost-command drill, the team is only capable of checking along the major routes off the location of lost command. There will be a number of places along those routes into which the target can possibly turn undetected. In residential areas or areas with few accesses in and out, the probability that the target will pass back through the location of lost command is greater. For this reason, the team may select to leave a commit surveillance vehicle at that location from the outset.

The rule of the team returning to box the point of lost command applies in a vacuum. If the team has information from previous observations of the target or another source to indicate where the target may have gone, the team may choose to move to that area in an attempt to reestablish command. The team may also determine that boxing the location of lost command will be futile and return to square one by placing a stakeout box on the target's residence.

FOOT SURVEILLANCE

To this point, the discussion of tactics has primarily focused on their application to vehicular surveillance. This is appropriate because most of these tactics apply in principle to foot surveillance as well. Since the majority of illegal or operational activity conducted by a given target can be expected to take place while on foot, foot surveillance is a critical aspect of virtually any operation.

Foot surveillance is normally employed as an element of a combined foot and vehicular surveillance operation. It is rare to have a target who does not either drive a vehicle, travel as a regular passenger, or travel by public transportation. In some cases, a team may employ a foot surveillance to cover a specific area in which the target is expected to conduct significant activity. This allows the team to concentrate most of its operators on the ground with only limited support from surveillance vehicles. Such circumstances are normally the result of credible information indicating that a concentrated foot surveillance will gain maximum results.

COMMUNICATIONS EQUIPMENT

Proper communications

equipment significantly enhances the effectiveness of a foot surveillance effort. Teams operating without communications equipment are restricted to the use of visual signals to communicate. This requires that the entire team maintain visual contact with the target or other team members. To accomplish this, the team must concentrate in the same vicinity as the target, thus risking security through the unnecessary exposure of operators to the target. Additionally, overt signals by foot operators are readily detectable by the target, countersurveillance, or pedestrians. With communications equipment, there is no need to maintain visual contact with other operators. This provides the team the flexibility to maneuver over a greater area in support of the operation with significantly less risk of detection.

When it is necessary to use visual signals, the team must be familiar with this type of communications system. Signals must be developed and practiced to cover every possible contingency of a foot surveillance. As the reader progresses through this and the next chapter, these possible contingencies will become clear. The visual signals developed to facilitate communications during a foot surveillance must appear natural to the casual observer. They should reflect common actions and mannerisms such as scratching one's head, checking one's watch, or removing a handkerchief from one's pocket.

An important aspect of using body communications equipment is mastering its use in a natural manner. Initially, such equipment may seem awkward, but as the operator becomes accustomed to the feel, it will appear natural. The equipment may require looser-fitting clothes, but nothing baggy and conspicuous in appearance. With the miniature microphone concealed near the center of the chest, the operator can talk in a very low tone and still be received by the team.

As the operator gains experience, it becomes easy to communicate on public streets without appearing to be talking to himself and drawing attention. One common error the operator must learn to avoid is the natural tendency to lower the chin when talking into the microphone. A good-quality microphone is sensitive enough to receive regardless of the position of the head. Recall that the key button will normally be run through a hole into the operator's pocket. The operator must master the skill of pushing the button to transmit without appearing as though fidgeting in his pocket.

Another initial tendency is for the operator to periodically feel his ear to ensure that the earpiece is still intact. Earpieces should be formfitting and checked in advance to ensure that they are inserted securely. A target who is suspicious of surveillance will certainly key on an individual with hand in pocket and finger in ear. Yet another tendency is for the operator to stop moving and stare aimlessly when listening to radio transmissions. Once again, all of these precautions regarding the use of body communications equipment will become second nature with experience.

Even when the team is concentrating its efforts on foot, surveillance vehicles should always accompany the team in support. The primary reason for this is that body communications systems have a limited range. This is particularly true in built-up urban areas where physical structures and a high volume of signals in the electromagnetic spectrum degrade communications. Vehicles equipped with power amplifiers transmit with much greater power than body communications equipment. A surveillance team that is effectively dispersed on the ground will normally need surveillance vehicles to relay the transmissions of one foot operator to other operators who are out of range. Additionally, surveillance vehicles can support the foot operators by transporting them around the operational area to optimize coverage. (These practices will be discussed in detail in Chapter 10.)

FOOT SURVEILLANCE PREPARATION

In preparation for a foot surveillance operation, the team should become familiar with the anticipated operational area. Primary streets, structures, and landmarks should be memorized when possible. Foot operators should orient such points of reference to the cardinal directions (north, south, east, west) in order to orient themselves when on the ground. Use of the sun to assist in orientation is an effective method but can be misleading during the middle of the day or when overcast. Maps can be miniaturized and carried in a concealed manner for reference when necessary, but the operator cannot depend on a map because the circumstances of the follow may not facilitate discreet use.

Surveillance operators should dress in a manner that blends with other people in the area. Shoes should be comfortable and quiet. Plenty of extra cash should be carried in anticipation of any possible operational requirement. This should include adequate change to use in pay telephones for both cover and to contact the team. If an operator experiences a failure in body communications equipment, a telephone may be his only means of contact with the team. If surveillance vehicles equipped with telephones are present in support, an operator can contact a surveillance vehicle to arrange a pickup or to be reoriented to the target's location. With surveillance vehicles in support, it may be more appropriate in some circumstances to observe the target from a phone booth and transmit information to a surveillance vehicle over the phone. The surveillance vehicle can in turn relay this information to the entire team over the radio.

The team should be familiar with all of the operators' names to be used on the radio. Foot operators will normally use operational names that are different from their true ones. This is primarily to ensure that if radio transmissions are intercepted by an individual or agency not affiliated with the team, no true information regarding the operators' identities will be compromised. Remember that even encrypted transmissions can be deciphered. Operational names should be one or two syllables long for brevity purposes and should also blend with the operational area.

If the team is restricted to operating without communications equipment, visual signals must be prearranged and thoroughly understood by all team members. A team operating without communications equipment should have a control base manned with a telephone. When possible during the surveillance operation, foot operators will telephone the base to provide the location and status of the target. This allows team members who become separated from the follow to telephone the base for the target's location in order to rejoin the follow. If a control base is not used, specified rendezvous points should be predetermined for operators who become separated from the follow.

FOOT SURVEILLANCE TACTICS

Most of the basic tactics discussed in vehicular surveillance apply on foot as well. The primary differences are slower speed of travel and increased flexibility in movement associated with foot surveillance. The slower speed of travel allows more time for the team to coordinate their actions. However, this slower speed also makes it more difficult to close distance on the target when necessary. Increased flexibility in movement is one of the greatest advantages that the team realizes during a foot surveillance. With a vehicular surveillance, the

)utes of travel are primarily restricted to established roads. By foot, :avel is generally less channelized, thus allowing the team to maneu- er with fewer obstacles. Of course, the target is also less restricted in iis options of travel.

Cover and Security

There will be varying degrees of cover in foot surveillance, depending on the time and location in which the operation takes place. Probably the most significant aspect of cover is traffic density. This consists primarily of the amount of pedestrian traffic on the streets. Foot operators will enhance their cover by acting and dress- ing in a manner that blends with the pedestrian traffic. Pedestrian traffic will also be used to physically obstruct the target's view of foot operators in a natural manner.

Physical structures such as buildings can be used for cover when employed properly. Foot operators should walk close to structures to take advantage of the shadows when appropriate. Any type of build- ing that has windows or outside visual access can be used by foot operators who are positioned inside and observing out. Foot opera- tors should avoid using physical structures to hide behind when it does not appear natural. They should avoid ducking behind or into a structure when the target turns or looks in their direction. Unnatural actions, such as peeking out from behind a structure, should also be avoided. All these actions are specifically what a surveillance-con- scious target will look for when attempting to detect surveillance.

When conducting a foot follow, each foot operator should con- stantly look ahead to assess potential cover opportunities. The opera- tor never knows when he will be exposed if the target makes an unexpected move. In such situations, the operator cannot make an abrupt or unnatural move. The operator must be aware of the cover opportunities available at any given time in order to make a natural transition from the follow to a cover position. If adequate cover does not exist, the operator should not stop or turn purposely when the target makes an unexpected maneuver. This, again, will be keyed on by the target. If necessary, the operator should continue naturally even when this results in passing or walking by the target.

Stakeout and Boxing Tactics

Increased maneuverability and time to maneuver is probably best exploited in the stakeout or surveillance box. Recall that in vehicular surveillance there are certain rules that dictate how a surveillance vehicle should be positioned for a box position. These rules are necessary because of the predominance of traffic obstacles and the difficulty of maneuvering a surveillance vehicle in a secure and timely manner. By foot, most of these obstacles do not exist. The only restrictions to a foot operator's ability to travel in any direction with equal ease are physical obstacles—and this restriction represents a constant variable for both the operator and the target.

The basic principles of the foot box are similar to those of the vehicular box. The stakeout box must cover the routes in and out of a specified area, and the surveillance box must cover all of the routes out of the area that the target is in. In many circumstances, cover for action is a greater concern for the foot operator. In a surveillance vehicle there is a degree of cover, both physical and plausible. On foot, an operator cannot stand aimlessly in the open to man a box position.

In residential and rural areas there is rarely adequate cover to support a foot stakeout of any duration. Long-range observation devices for greater stand-off distance are generally more effective when the target is on foot in rural areas. Directional microphones can also be effective for listening to conversations in such an environment when little noise interference exists. Fortunately, foot surveillances are not common in rural areas. Most foot surveillance operations will occur in built-up urban areas where more than adequate cover is available to the resourceful operator.

Metropolitan areas provide a number of good opportunities to establish box positions or static positions to observe the target. Any store, restaurant, or other appropriate establishment with windows facing the location to be observed can be used as a box position. An operator positioned to look out a window and onto the street he is supposed to observe has perfect cover from the target as he passes. The same operator cannot man such a box position indefinitely, however. If the same location is best for that specific box assignment, another operator can be discreetly rotated in to replace the operator who has worn out his welcome or become conspicuous.

When using a restaurant for cover to sit and observe a position from inside, the operator should pay as he is served to avoid having to settle with the cashier while the target walks away. Also, large meals should be avoided because the operator may be forced to move before the meal is finished or even served. Individuals who pay for a meal without eating appear suspicious to countersurveillance and unwitting restaurant employees alike.

Locations such as telephone booths, park benches, and bus stops make adequate locations for short-term box positions. This type of cover must be employed in a natural manner. Any individual who stays at a bus stop for an extended period while buses come and go will appear suspicious before long. Countersurveillance detection is always a threat, but bus drivers who see the same person at a stop on their second pass may become concerned. An operator who is approached by police as a loiterer or possible mugger waiting for a mark is an unnecessary and avoidable security risk. In the same vein, an operator cannot carry on a telephone conversation indefinitely without appearing suspicious. If an operator uses a phone booth for cover in a box position, then it must appear realistic. The operator can call a surveillance vehicle or the control base, but he must be talking with someone to project a natural appearance to any third persons who may be observing or the target who may happen by at anytime. Anyone who stands at length and talks into a dead phone will risk drawing attention.

One primary difference between the vehicular stakeout box and the foot stakeout is that, by foot, the team does not wait for the target to break the box before maneuvering. Recall that with the vehicular stakeout, when the target enters the box the team waits until the target breaks out of the box before beginning the follow. This is done because, in a vehicular follow, the routes of travel are channelized by the roads, and there is nowhere for the target to drive his vehicle except out of the box on one of those roads. By foot, however, the target will normally have more options of travel while in the box. For this reason it is important for a foot operator to establish command of the target as soon as possible. Additionally, the foot operator has much more flexibility to move quickly in any direction than does a surveillance vehicle.

FOOT OPERATOR POSITIONING

As the target is picked up, the operator in the best position will establish command and inform the team of such. As the target and the command operator pass any subsequent box positions, the operators manning those positions will fall in behind and enter the follow. The first operator to join the command operator in the follow will establish a backing position similar to that of a vehicular follow. The backing operator will notify the command that he is backing, and the follow will proceed.

During the follow, the command operator can be positioned on either side of the road or route of travel. When there is no backing operator, it is normally more effective for the command operator to be on the same side of the road as the target. This is only the case because, when on the same side of the road, the operator will be confronted only with the same

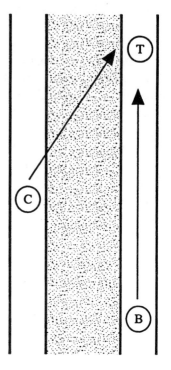

FIGURE 20

obstacles as the target. On the opposite side of the road, the operator may be forced to attempt to maneuver across the road through traffic or other obstacles to maintain command of the target. If the operator is obstructed from crossing the road when necessary, command of the target may be lost.

When there is a backing operator, it is ideal for the command operator to be on the opposite side of the road from the target. Unless there is a significant amount of vehicular traffic that obstructs the view of the command operator, the opposite side of the road will usually give a better angle of observation. When following directly behind the target, pedestrian traffic is more apt to obstruct the command operator's vision. Additionally, a target who is observing for surveillance is more likely to look directly to his rear rather than across the road and back. If the target suddenly reverses his direction, a command operator on the opposite side of the road will not be exposed by this maneuver.

In many cases the circumstances of the follow will dictate which side of the road the command operator is on. The command operator should not cross the road to correct his position unless it is necessary to continue the follow within the parameters of security. During a straight follow, it should never be necessary for the command operator to cross the road when there is a backing operator. The backing operator should always follow on the opposite side of the road as the command operator. This very important tactic allows the command/backing operator tandem to overcome traffic obstacles by covering for each other.

In dense traffic, the backing operator may close distance to the point that he is directly parallel to the command operator. Whatever the distance may be between the command and backing operators, this positioning gives them a combined field of vision that enables greater dual command of the target. In dense traffic where there are many obstacles to interfere with line of sight, these two operators may volley command of the target back and forth between themselves. Figure 20 depicts the standard command operator (C) and backing operator (B) positioning.

One factor that allows the team more flexibility in executing the previous tactics, as well as many others, is a slower rate of speed that provides the team more time to coordinate its activities. Another significant factor that allows the team more flexibility is that the target can only see to his rear by physically turning around. This flexibility does not exist during a vehicular follow because the target can observe following traffic through his rear-view mirror at any time without any overt indication. Communications equipment allows the foot surveillance team to exploit this increased degree of flexibility to the maximum.

During the foot follow, the operators other than the command and backing operators will maneuver as appropriate to support the follow. There should always be at least one other operator following the backing operator in order to assume the latter's responsibilities when he establishes command of the target. This third operator should be positioned on the opposite side of the road as the backing operator. This will ensure that when the backing operator establishes command of the target, the other operator can establish a backing position from which it can execute the follow, as previously discussed.

Command/Backing Foot Operator Coordination

As previously discussed, the command and backing foot operators have more flexibility in coordinating and exchanging command of the target. One area where coordination is critical to the exchange of command is at blind turns. Blind turns are options such as intersections or other foot routes at which the target may turn, causing the command operator to lose sight of the target. Blind turns are particularly characteristic of urban areas where buildings line the sidewalk on virtually every block.

Probably the oldest yet most effective method of surveillance detection is for the target to turn a blind corner and stop. The target will then observe the individuals who also turn the corner, attempting to pick out anyone who appears startled or turns his head and walks by stoically. Even an operator who maintains his composure when confronted with such a situation will be exposed, thus facilitating future recognition by the target.

To counter the threat that a target may use this detection tactic at any blind corner, the command and backing operators must coordinate their actions for security, as well as command, purposes. The method used to accomplish this is referred to as *corner clearing*. Corner clearing is a tactic whereby one operator continues straight past the blind corner taken by the target. As that operator passes the location of the turn, he will glance to ensure that the target has continued through the turn in a normal manner. If the target has continued on, the operator will inform the team that the corner is clear while continuing straight through the location of the turn. If the target has stopped, the operator will inform the team that the corner is not clear, while continuing straight.

The tactic of corner clearing is executed by the command and backing operators. At the instant that the target takes a blind turn, the command operator must decide whether he will clear the corner or direct the backing operator to clear the corner. Recall that if the command and backing operators are positioned correctly, one will be on each side of the road. When both the command and backing operators are on the same side of the road, the command operator has no choice but to clear the corner for the backing operator. This is less than ideal because it restricts the team from taking advantage of the terrain and situation. This point will become clear as the advantages of corner clearing with the command and backing operators properly positioned are explained.

When the command and backing operators are positioned on opposite sides of the road, the command operator has the flexibility to determine how the corner can be cleared most securely and effectively. This determination will be based primarily on two factors—the amount of cover and the number of traffic obstacles at the location of the turn.

Probably the most critical consideration will be traffic obstacles that could obstruct an operator from crossing the road to establish command of the target. If there is a significant possibility that traffic would have such an effect, the command operator will normally determine that the operator on the side of the road that is opposite the target should clear the corner. Depending on which side of the road the command operator is on in relation to the target, this could be him or it may be the backing operator. The operator on the opposite side of the road should clear the corner because he might not be able to cross the street to establish command if the operator on the same side as the target were the one to clear.

Figure 21 depicts the command operator (C) clearing the corner for the backing operator (B). After the command operator clears the corner, the backing operator will turn the corner to establish command of the target. Note that the backing operator can either turn directly behind the target or cross the street and turn. Crossing the street will place the operator in the best command position, but this may not be possible due to traffic obstacles.

Figure 22 is a follow-up to the previous figure. It depicts how the next operator in the follow changes into the backing operator position after the exchange of command is complete. The side of the road that the new backing operator selects is dictated by which side the new command operator selected during the exchange. The backing operator will maneuver to the side of the road opposite the command operator, regardless of the target's position.

Enhanced security is another advantage in having the operator on the opposite side of the road clear the corner. If the operator on the same side of the road as the target is the one to clear the corner, he may still be vulnerable to the turn-and-stop method of surveillance detection. Being on the same side of the road may place him too close to the target as he glances to clear the corner. Despite the team's effort to maintain security by clearing the corner, this may still

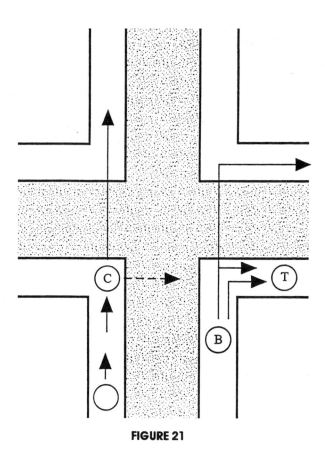

FIGURE 21

appear suspicious to a witting target. The operator on the opposite side of the street, however, can clear the corner from a greater distance, thus minimizing the risk of detection.

As with vehicular surveillance, it is always a risk to security to take a corner directly behind the target. When the command operator determines that he must exchange command of the target because of security reasons, factors such as cover and traffic obstacles become academic. Remember that it is always better to make a decision that risks losing the target rather than compromising the operation. In a team follow with a backing operator, it is not necessary to take such security risks unless there is excellent cover.

Cover in foot surveillances will primarily consist of pedestrian traffic. When traffic obstacles are not a significant factor in deter-

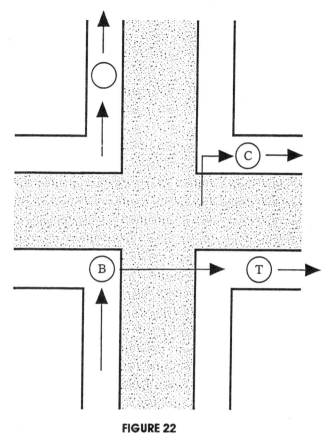

FIGURE 22

mining which operator is in the best position to clear the corner,
the command operator is free to base this determination strictly on
cover. The disadvantage of having the operator on the same side of
the road as the target clear the corner has been addressed.

The risk here is that the operator may still be too close if the
target has stopped after turning the corner. If there is little or no
cover, however, it may be a greater risk to turn the corner on the
same side of the road as the target, even after having the corner
cleared. This is an advantage to having the operator on the same
side of the road as the target clear the corner for the operator on
the opposite side. If there are no significant traffic obstacles, the
opposite side operator is in a more secure position to turn and cross
the street to establish command of the target. The possibility of

additional cover is also more likely from this position.

If additional cover is not available in the form of pedestrian traffic, then the greater stand-off distance from the target alone will make it a more secure position. Figure 23 depicts the backing operator (B) clearing the corner for the command operator (C). After the backing operator clears the corner and continues straight, the command operator turns the corner to establish command of the target. Note again that the command operator can turn and follow on the same side of the road as the target or can cross the road at the intersection to turn and follow on the opposite side of the road. Again, this determination will be influenced by traffic obstacles.

In situations where there is adequate cover, the command operator can clear a corner for himself without a backing operator. As the target turns the corner, the command operator will continue past the point of the turn and clear the corner. He will then cross the street and turn in the same direction as the target on the opposite side of the road (Figure 24).

This tactic can be executed regardless of which side of the road the command operator is on prior to the target taking the turn. The only disadvantage to executing this tactic from the opposite side of the road from the target is that the operator must negotiate traffic obstacles in crossing two roads. This may be difficult on large, busy intersections. At such intersections, however, the operator may have sufficient cover to clear the corner for himself while only crossing one road. When the target takes a turn, the operator will continue to the intersection without crossing. While checking the traffic at the intersection as any pedestrian would, the operator will look in the direction of the target to ensure that he has continued around the corner in a normal manner. If this is the case, the operator can then cross the road in the direction of the target and continue the follow on the same side of the road (Figure 25).

At large, busy intersections, the command and backing operators can also use variations of the previous examples to clear the corner for each other. The advantage in doing so is that the operator who clears the corner is not forced to continue straight after the intersection, thus taking himself out of the follow. Figure 26 depicts the command operator (C) clearing the corner for the backing operator (B), while still continuing in the follow.

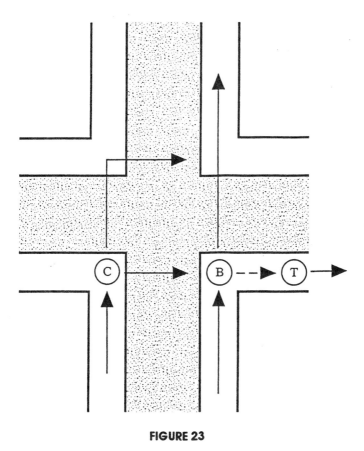

FIGURE 23

Figure 27 depicts the backing operator (B) clearing the corner for the command operator (C), while still continuing in the follow. In this situation, the backing operator will become the command operator because of his positioning on the opposite side of the road as the target.

One might ask why an operator cannot just continue straight through the intersection and then use the cover of buildings to reverse direction, return to the intersection, and continue along with the follow. This is effective in keeping the operator directly involved with the follow, but it is not a sound tactic for any surveillance team that is concerned about countersurveillance. Additionally, if the target were to observe an operator continue through an intersection, disappear, and then come back to the

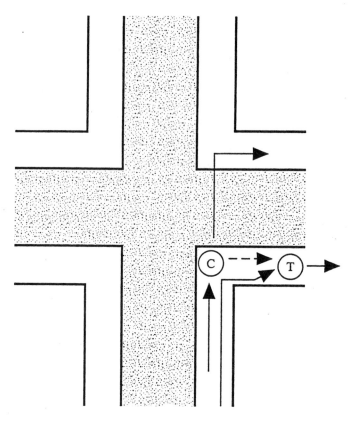

FIGURE 24

intersection and travel in the target's direction, the team can consider its operation compromised at that point. In addition to the previous point, recall from the discussion of vehicular surveillance that there is an advantage, other than security, to an operator continuing through the intersection after exchanging command. This advantage is that it places the operator in a perfect position to continue to the next intersection and take up a parallel route. This is a natural pattern through which the foot surveillance can mature from a straight follow to the floating box.

FLOATING BOX

The increased degree of flexibility in maneuvering and time to

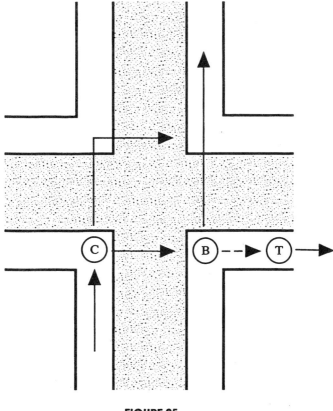

FIGURE 25

coordinate actions during a foot surveillance make the floating box a particularly effective tactic. Recall that in the discussion of vehicular surveillance, the floating box was introduced as a method by which the team can disperse its positions to more effectively overcome obstacles encountered by the surveillance vehicles following the same route as the target. The floating box follows the same principles employed during the foot follow. The increased maneuverability and less channelized terrain provide the foot team many more parallel routes to exploit. When the foot team is conducting the follow and has established the floating box, this will be of significant importance if the target goes unsighted. Figure 28 depicts the command operator (C) at the location of lost command and indicates the target's last known direction of travel.

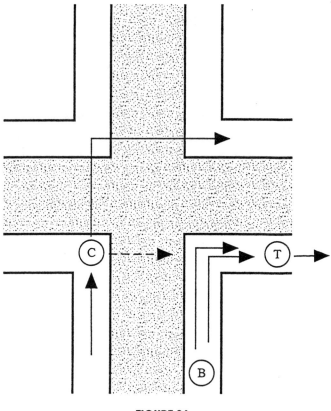

FIGURE 26

In this situation, the floating box will simply collapse in toward the location where the target was last observed. The foot operators on the north and south parallels will collapse the floating box to search for the target. Since there is not an operator boxing ahead, the (formerly) command operator must check the target's last known direction of travel. If the operators reach the point where the target was last seen with negative results and the (formerly) command operator has checked his route to the limit of time-distance with negative results, then the team can be fairly certain that the target entered a building or establishment along one of those routes. The operators will then backtrack and begin checking the possible locations the target could have entered along their designated route.

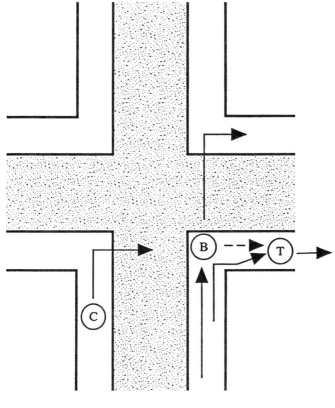

FIGURE 27

LOST-COMMAND DRILL

The previous section discussed how the floating box can be collapsed to conduct a lost-command drill. The team cannot rely, however, on having a floating box established to facilitate each lost-command drill. The lost-command drill conducted when the target goes unsighted during the straight follow is similar to that discussed in Chapter 7.

Operators will check logical routes of travel away from the location that the target was last sighted. The mathematical equation of the time-distance formula does not apply in foot surveillance, but all operators will check for the target along their designated routes until they judge that—based on time-distance—the target did not travel that far along their routes. At that point, the operator will inform the

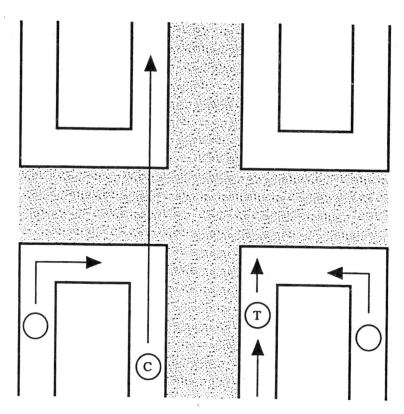

FIGURE 28

team of the negative results of the check, then turn to retrace the route in the direction of the location of lost command.

As the operators return, they will begin to check inside establishments along their routes that the target may have entered undetected. Because of the slower rate of speed that the target is traveling in a foot surveillance, the team has the flexibility to check establishments in the area more thoroughly. The team must place a priority on having an operator establish a control position at the location of lost command if this was not done at the outset. If the target returns to the location of lost command, the control operator will be able to inform the team and pick up the target. The slower rate of speed should allow the other operators to recover and join the follow in a reasonable amount of time.

SURVEILLANCE IN PUBLIC LOCATIONS

A public location is any area or establishment that provides open access to the public. Public locations are differentiated from public streets because they normally have physical or notional boundaries and a greater concentration of people. The number of public locations to which a target may lead the surveillance team is unlimited. They consist of such places as restaurants, stores, malls, parks, or airports. The greater concentration of people and the presence of boundaries impose unique restrictions on foot operators. In most cases, public locations force the operators much closer to the target than they would otherwise allow themselves to be.

The previous chapter addressed the basic foot surveillance tactics. Although they are less than ideal, many of the tactics discussed can be executed without the support of communications equipment. Public locations completely detach an operator or operators from the rest of the team. Without communications equipment, an operator is isolated with the target to one degree or another and must operate independently. Any observations of the target will not support the surveillance in progress because they do not benefit any other operators and will probably not be detailed to the rest of the team until after the operation is terminated. Of course, any observations of a target that support the objectives of an operation are important whether or not they are immediately transmitted to the team.

This chapter will first discuss public locations and the tactics employed by a team with body communications equipment. After these specific applications are addressed, unique locations and circumstances that the surveillance operator may confront will be explained.

PUBLIC LOCATION ASSESSMENT

The first factor an operator should consider when entering a public location with the target is the objectives of the operation. If the objectives are to determine all activities and contacts of the target, then it will probably be necessary to enter such locations with the target. If the objective is only to determine general travel patterns of the target, then the team will probably not risk exposure by entering public locations with the target.

The next factor an operator will consider when making this determination is the amount of cover available in the public location. When this assessment has been made, the operator will make a judgment of whether to enter based on an understanding of the objectives as discussed above. The operator will normally have to make an immediate judgment as to whether, based on the degree of cover, the potential payoff from entering the location outweighs the risk of exposure to or compromise by the target. In some cases the operator will not be able to make such an assessment from outside the public location. In this case, the operator must base his determination of whether to enter strictly on the objectives of the operation. Some public locations such as parks and malls provide adequate cover to make the decision an easy one. Other locations such as cafes or small bars make the decision a difficult one. In some cases, the objectives of the operation will dictate that an operator enter a confined location with the target.

The operator may enter a location knowing that the resulting degree of exposure to the target will disqualify him automatically from any further operations against that target. This, however, is the price that must be paid in order to develop critical information in support of the operation's objectives.

In addition to the previously discussed considerations, the operator must be aware of the fact that a sophisticated target may enter public locations to facilitate surveillance detection. This is an effective tactic because it allows the target to isolate surveillance operators in a confined area for identification purposes. Also, the presence of electronic security devices at the entrance of a public location may be a discriminating factor in determining whether to enter. An operator should never enter a location with an electronic monitoring system when carrying a firearm. More sensitive systems may detect the presence of body communications equipment, but the large majority will not. In any case, the electromagnetic emissions from the system will interfere with the effectiveness of the communications to some degree.

When an operator elects to enter a public location with the target, he will inform the team of his intentions. Unless it is a location that obviously has sufficient cover to facilitate more than one operator, no other operators will enter the location until the operator entering with the target reestablishes command of the target and reports the status. As the operator enters a public location with the target, he must immediately establish cover for action—a reason for being there. This is as simple as blending with the other individuals in the location. If it is a store, then shop. If it is a restaurant, then sit and order. The operator must not, however, forget the reason that he is in there while establishing cover. The reason, of course, is to observe the activities of the target.

There is certain information the operator must transmit to the team as soon as possible after entering the location. Some of the information is important to begin transmitting even before establishing command of the target if possible. The reader may question how the operator will be able to transmit all of this information in a public location and perhaps even within voice range of the target. A subsequent section will explain how an operator with body communications equipment can transmit information to the team without saying a word. The pertinent information that the operator must provide to the team is as follows:

• *Command Established.* It is important for the operator to inform the team the instant that he has established command of the target. Knowing that the operator will be able to inform the team when the target is about to exit the location allows the team to establish a more deliberate box, as opposed to a hasty one. The operator will attempt to provide the team information regarding the target's location and activities inside the public location.

• *Target Making Contact.* If the target is making contact with another individual inside a public location, this will take priority over all other information to be transmitted. This is because the team may select to designate the person in contact as the primary target of the surveillance in order to identify this individual. The operator will provide as much descriptive information regarding the contact as possible. This will allow the team to recognize the individual if he becomes the target of the surveillance. The operator will then attempt to assess the purpose of the contact to assist the team in determining whether that individual needs to be identified. All pertinent information regarding the contact should be transmitted. If the operator is unable to transmit detailed information for security reasons, then he must be certain to recall all of the content, to include listening to any conversation if possible. The operator must also make keen observations regarding the contact's appearance. This is critical because if the team is unable to attain an identification-quality photograph of the contact, then the operator will need to produce a composite picture after the operation. The operator will use his judgment regarding contacts that appear consequential, such as a waitress taking the target's order. These contacts do not have to be reported at the time but must be remembered to ensure that the surveillance report contains complete details.

• *Length of Stay.* The operator will make an assessment of how long it appears that the target will remain inside the location. By transmitting this information to the team, this again provides an indicator of how long the members have to establish their box around the location. Sometimes this is a subjective judgment on the part of the operator. In other cases, it is an easy one. For example, if the target enters a restaurant and sits to order, then it is safe to assume that it will be a long stay.

• *If the Operator Needs Help.* The operator will inform the team if he needs help inside the location. The location may be large enough, such as a department store, that he needs additional operators inside to help maintain command of the target. In a restaurant the operator may request that another operator join him to eat, thus enhancing his cover. This is a particularly effective tactic in allowing the operator to transmit information more securely to the team. With a partner along, the operator can transmit information to the team while appearing to engage in casual conversation. Whatever the case may be, the operator will inform the team of the reason that he needs help, so that any additional operators can enter the location in a natural manner and establish immediate cover for action.

• *If the Target Can Observe Outside.* The operator inside the public location will inform the team of the target's vantage point and ability to observe activity outside the location. This information will indicate to the team the degree of freedom they have to maneuver around outside of the location without being observed by the target.

• *Number of Exits to the Location.* When a target enters a public location, the number and locations of additional exits to that location may not be immediately apparent to the operators outside. In built-up areas and shopping centers, there may be exits that cannot be identified through outside examination. For this reason it is important that the operator inside attempt to determine the number and location of the exits. This information is necessary for the team to establish a box with no holes.

• *If the Target Can Observe the Exit(s).* This information complements the information regarding the number and location of the exits. It provides the team with information regarding which exit, if any, is the most secure by which additional operators may enter the location.

• *If the Operator Will Observe the Target Exit.* When the operator is able to observe the target exit the location, the team is assured that there will be a direct exchange of command when this occurs. There are some situations in which the operator is able to observe the activities of the target while inside the public location, but the operator is committed to a position that will not allow him to observe the target exit. This is common in restaurants where the operator is seated in a position to observe the target but will lose command when the target leaves his table. This informs the team that there will be a period in which the target will go unsighted before exiting the location. Based on this information, the team may select to send another operator in to establish a trigger position on the exit.

SILENT COMMUNICATIONS PRACTICES

There are many situations, to include public locations, that the surveillance operator will encounter difficulties in transmitting voice communications because of the risk of being heard. This applies not only to being overheard by the target, but anybody in the area. Most public locations have clientele or employees who are sensitive to suspicious individuals or potential criminal activities. Many locations have dedicated security personnel for this purpose.

In situations where the surveillance operator must transmit critical information but voice transmissions are not practical, the voiceless system of communication can be used. The voiceless system relies on a second operator, or interrogator, to ask quesitons of the operator in the public location. When the transmitter button of the body communications system is pressed, it will transmit static if nothing is said. This enables the surveillance operator in a public location to communicate information to the entire team by sending static transmissions in response to the interrogator's questions.

The principle of the voiceless system is that the interrogator will ask the operator questions that mirror the types of important information the entire team needs to have, as discussed in the previous section. The operator will answer the interrogator's questions by either transmitting two clicks for an affirmative response or transmitting nothing for a negative response. When the interrogator gets a negative response to a question, he will ask the same question again in the negative form in order to get an affirmative response. This is done to ensure that the operator did in fact hear the question. This conceptual description may be confusing at this point but will become clear as the practical applications are discussed.

The operator in the public location and the interrogator should have priority on the radio network. It is ideal to have the interrogation conducted from a surveillance vehicle whenever possible. This process requires that the interrogator ask a number of questions in quick succession. A surveillance vehicle provides a secure location for the interrogator to operate without as much risk of being overheard or interrupted. A surveillance vehicle's communications system can transmit with much more power than the communications system of a foot operator. This will make it easier for the operator being interrogated to hear the questions. Additionally, the surveillance vehicle can relay the information from the operator to other members of the team who are otherwise out of range of the operator in the public location or to another foot operator conducting the interrogation.

Normally, the voiceless system will be initiated by the operator after entering the public location with the target. The operator will probably have nothing important to transmit until after he has established command of the target. The operator will initiate the interrogation with a steady rush of static or multiple clicks. At that point the interrogator will begin the systematic process of questioning. Recall that the interrogator will first ask a question in the affirmative form. Affirmative-form questions that receive no answer are reworded in the negative form to ensure an affirmative response to one of the questions. For the purposes of this example, an operator named Drake has entered a public location behind the target. The interrogation process is as follows:

Drake: Multiple clicks or steady rush of static
Interrogator: Is that Drake?
Drake: Two clicks (affirmative response)
Interrogator: Drake, are you in command?
Drake: Two clicks (affirmative response)
Interrogator: Drake, is the target in contact?
(This asks if the target is meeting another individual.)
Drake: No clicks (possible negative response)
Interrogator: Drake, is the target not in contact?
Drake: Two clicks (affirmative response)

Notice that when the interrogator received a possible negative response in the form of nothing transmitted from the operator, he reworded the question in the negative form by adding the word not. By doing this, the operator was able to make it clear to the team that the target was not in contact. This ensures that miscommunication or the operator's being unable to respond at that particular instant is not mistaken for a negative response.

When the target is in contact with an individual, the interrogator will ask questions to elicit a description of that individual. The interrogator will also elicit specific information regarding the contact in order to determine whether identification of that individual should become a primary objective of the operation.

If the interrogator gets no response (possible negative response) to both forms of the question, then he will ask a third form of the question. The interrogator cannot discount the possibility that by giving two negative responses, the operator simply does not know the answer to the question. To determine whether this is the case, a third form of the question must be asked. This is done as follows:

Interrogator: Drake, does it look like a long stay?
Drake: No clicks (possible negative response)
Interrogator: Drake, does it not look like a long stay?
Drake: No clicks (possible negative response)
Interrogator: Drake, do you not know if it looks
    like a long stay?
Drake: Two clicks (affirmative response)

By asking this third form of the question, the operator was able to inform the team that he is not sure how long the target will remain in the public location. This informs the team that the target could exit at any time with little warning. If the interrogator gets a negative response to all three forms of the question, he must assume that the operator did not hear the questions or was unable to respond. When this occurs, the interrogator will ensure that the operator can still hear his transmissions. If this were the case, the interrogator would ask:

Interrogator: Drake, can you hear me?

If nothing is heard the interrogator will repeat the question. If there is still no response from the operator, the interrogator must assume that he has lost communications. At that point, the interrogator will request that another operator or surveillance vehicle with a better vantage point attempt to reestablish communications with the operator. If no other operator or surveillance vehicle is able to establish communications with the operator in the public location, they must maneuver to a position that facilitates a communications link. They must also be aware of the fact that the target may exit the public location at any time with no warning. Since the foot operators outside the public location have been establishing a box while the interrogation has been taking place, this should not be an insurmountable problem. Having discussed contingency questions and tactics, the interrogation format will continue as though the interrogator has communications with the operator.

Interrogator: Drake, does target have a good look out?
Drake: Two clicks (affirmative response)
Interrogator: Drake, is there only one exit?
Drake: No clicks (possible negative response)
Interrogator: Drake, is there not only one exit?
Drake: Two clicks (affirmative response)
Interrogator: Drake, are there two exits?
Drake: Two clicks (affirmative response)

Now the interrogator must determine where the other exit is.

Interrogator: Drake, we are aware of the front exit.
　Is the second exit to the rear?
Drake: No clicks (possible negative response)
Interrogator: Drake, is the second exit not to the rear?
Drake: Two clicks (affirmative response)
Interrogator: Drake, is the second exit to the right of
　the front exit?

This question is asked from the vantage point of someone on the outside looking in. All operators must know in advance that this is the perspective from which the question will asked, to avoid any confusion.

Drake: Two clicks (affirmative response)
Interrogator: Drake, does target have a good look
   at the front exit?
Drake: Two clicks (affirmative response)
Interrogator: Drake, does target have a good
   look at the side exit?
Drake: No clicks (possible negative response)
Interrogator: Drake, does target not have a
   good look at the side exit?
Drake: Two clicks (affirmative response)
Interrogator: Drake, do you need help?
Drake: Two clicks (affirmative response)
Interrogator: Drake, do you need help to command target?
Drake: No clicks (possible negative response)
Interrogator: Drake, do you not need help to command target?
Drake: Two clicks (affirmative response)
Interrogator: Drake, do you need help for cover?
Drake: Two clicks (affirmative response)
Interrogator: Drake, Katie is on the way. Should
   Katie enter through the side door?
Drake: Two clicks (affirmative response)

Note that a female operator was sent to join the male operator. It will normally appear more natural for male and female
operators to dine or interact socially than would two males. At
this point the interrogator will ask any questions the operator was
previously unable to answer.

Interrogator: Drake, does it look like a long stay?
Drake: Two clicks (affirmative response)
Interrogator: Drake, do you have anything else to tell me?
Drake: No clicks (possible negative response)
Interrogator: Drake, do you not have anything else to tell me?
Drake: Two clicks (affirmative response)

At this point the initial portion of the interrogation is complete. The interrogator will retransmit all the information to the

entire team, for the benefit of those who were out of range to hear the operator's transmissions. Note that the last question asked was whether the operator had any additional information to provide the team. An affirmative response to this question is the greatest challenge the interrogator will encounter. Such a situation will require that the interrogator narrow down the possibilities to elicit the information. The possibilities can be limitless, but the three general questions to ask in an attempt to narrow the scope are

1) "Do you want to tell me something about target?" If no,
2) "Do you want to tell me about someone else inside?" If no,
3) "Do you want to tell me something about the building (public location)?"

If the operator wants to tell the team about someone else in the public location, the first follow-on question will be whether he suspects countersurveillance. If the interrogator is unable to narrow the scope based on these three questions, then the interrogator must be resourceful in determining what the operator wants to communicate. Other operators may interject their ideas in an effort to assist the interrogator in eliciting the information.

After the initial interrogation is complete, the operator will inform the interrogator when he has new information to transmit through a rapid series of clicks or a rush of static. The interrogator will, however, contact the operator approximately once every 10 minutes to ensure that there is still a communications link. When the operator gives the indication that there is information to transmit, the first question the interrogator will ask is "Is target intending to leave?" If the response to this question is affirmative, then the team will be on alert for the pickup. In this particular situation, the interrogator would ask the operator which exit the target is intending to use. If the response to the initial question is negative, then the next question that the interrogator will ask is "Is the target in contact?" If the response to this question is affirmative, then the interrogation will continue to attain information regarding the contact. If the response is negative, the interrogator will refer back to the above three scope-narrowing questions in an attempt to determine what information the operator wants to provide the team.

BOXING PUBLIC LOCATIONS

When establishing a box around a public location the target has entered, the team will follow the same principles of boxing as previously discussed. The box must be established quickly because the target may exit at any time, and perhaps by a different door from that he used to enter. The box will be established to ensure that when the target exits the public location, the team is able to execute a smooth pickup and follow. Foot operators will exercise quick judgment and initiative in selecting and maneuvering to an appropriate box position. All operators will inform the team of their intentions to avoid duplication of effort.

If the interrogation of an operator inside the public location is ongoing, the radio network must remain clear for the interrogator and command operator. Foot operators will not, however, delay their movement to box positions because there is an ongoing interrogation. When there is a break in the interrogation, an operator who has not already done so will inform the team of his location and intentions.

The first priority in the box is to establish a trigger on the door or entrance the target used to enter the public location. This is necessary because the entrance the target uses to enter will most likely be the one through which he will exit. The next priority is to determine where the other exits, if any, are located. As additional exits are located, they should be covered by trigger operators. Recall how an operator inside the public location can assist in determining the location of other exits.

After the exits have been located and covered, the remaining operators will establish appropriate control positions to facilitate the pickup and follow. In public locations with multiple exits, foot operators will prioritize their positions based on the most likely exit(s) from which the target will emerge. The team should, however, be positioned to execute a pickup from any exit to the location, regardless of how unlikely its use may appear. Of course, there are buildings that have too many exits for the team to cover. This is why large buildings are commonly used by a target for antisurveillance purposes. In such situations the team must either continue the follow into the building or accept the risk of not covering all the exits. A resourceful team will assess the interior of the building and establish box positions inside that cover the routes to multiple exits.

When the team is not using body communication equipment, the operator inside the public location cannot provide information to support the team's box positioning. Since they cannot expect to be alerted when the target departs, the team must cover the location as though there were no operators inside. An operator inside the public location may be able to communicate with surveillance vehicles or a control base by telephone, if either of these capabilities exists. In any case, this will likely fail to provide real-time information to the operators outside the location in box positions.

THE FOLLOW IN PUBLIC LOCATIONS

A team operating without communications equipment will generally be more aggressive in continuing a follow into a public location with multiple operators. By continuing the follow inside, the team is better able to maintain integrity through visual contact with the target or each other. When a team boxes a public location without body communications equipment, team integrity is normally degraded during the pickup because some operators will not observe or be alerted to the target's activities. Body communications equipment provides the team flexibility to commit only those operators necessary to conduct the follow inside the public location, thus minimizing the probability of exposing multiple operators.

There are a number of public locations large enough to facilitate a foot follow using multiple operators. The target can take a team to locations such as a zoo, ballpark, or shopping mall. These locations, however, are extremely dangerous for the surveillance team because of the restricted operating space. Such locations have a number of natural 180-degree turns that the target can use for surveillance detection purposes. Even if the target is not consciously practicing surveillance detection, the chances of unexpected moves are much greater in public locations.

A possibility that exists during all phases of a foot surveillance, but is much more likely in public locations, is that of eye contact. When a target makes eye contact with an operator, it will tend to make a more lasting impression in the target's memory, conscious or subconscious. For this reason, it is always important for the operator to avoid placing himself in a situation where eye contact is possible. In some circumstances this may not be possible.

When confronted in a face-to-face with the target, the operator must not make a noticeable effort to avoid eye contact. This will only make the target suspicious. In the event of eye contact, the operator at that point will have to make a realistic judgment as to whether he should be involved in future operations against the target. As stated previously, the objectives of the operation may dictate that an operator place himself in such a situation. It is always much better to lose one operator than to compromise the operation by allowing that operator to continue and be recognized at a later time.

During the course of a follow in a public location, it is not necessarily damaging if the target observes the same operator in more than one location. In a shopping mall, for example, it is not at all uncommon to see the same person more than once, as long as the person appears natural. A determination of whether an operator is a security risk to the operation after that portion of the follow will be based on the judgment of that operator.

An important aspect to the terrain of a follow in public locations is that it is three-dimensional. Not necessarily in the standard sense, rather in the sense that it expands up and down as well as out. This is an advantage in many situations but a disadvantage in most. Multilevel shopping malls, for example, are very favorable for foot follows. One or two operators strategically placed on the level above the target can command his actions in the main walking areas while directing operators to specific stores that the target enters. This is but one example of how an operator can use elevation to establish a static observation position from which to command the target over a distance.

Staircases and Elevators

Staircases and elevators represent particularly difficult obstacles for the foot operator. An operator on either of these with the target is isolated. Staircases are extremely difficult to follow on without detection. In fact, stairs are excellent locations for the target to conduct surveillance detection. An operator who follows the target up or down enclosed multilevel staircases and then exits behind the target is certain to draw attention.

Additionally, in many cases the operator will not know what type of situation he will encounter when he exits the staircase. In most situations, it will be best to continue on the stairs past the exit the target takes and inform the team of which level the target is on. The team can then approach the floor from different staircases, if available, and attempt to locate the target.

When the target enters an elevator, the operator must decide whether the objectives of the operation warrant certain exposure. Some elevators have floor lights outside that identify the level at which the elevator stops for people to either enter or exit. This can only provide some assistance in determining which level the target exits the elevator, particularly if there are other people on the elevator. If the operator determines that it is necessary to follow the target onto an elevator, he will likely draw the target's attention if he exits on the same floor. This may be necessary and can be executed securely if the operator is resourceful in establishing cover for action immediately upon exiting the elevator.

In situations when the operator enters an elevator and there are few or no other people to use as cover, the operator must assume that he has been exposed to the extent that only a complete disguise will allow him to continue in the operation. When this point is reached, the operator can take a more overt stance in determining the level at which the target will exit the elevator. In such situations, the operator can enter the elevator close to the level control buttons and immediately push the next-to-the-top-level button.

Then, while depressing his microphone key, he will ask the target which level he would like pushed. This will transmit the elevator level to the rest of the team by use of the target's voice. If the target selects the next-to-the-top level as well, the operator's cover is established because he selected that level before the target. Another method of transmitting the level selected by the target to the team is to press the microphone button the same number of times as that of the level chosen.

Restaurants

When the target enters a restaurant, the following operator

should allow time for the target to be seated before doing the same. This allows the operator to select an appropriate location to sit based on the location of the target. When seating is determined by a restaurant host, the operator may have to be resourceful in manipulating the situation. When the operator assesses that the probability of being seated where he can observe the target is low, he may select to be seated in a location that will at least allow him to observe the exit. This is easily done by the operator informing the host that he is expecting a companion and would like to be able to see the door.

When the operator is able to sit in a location that facilitates observation of the target, he should sit in a manner that allows him a clear view without being readily visible to the target. When the target is eating with another individual, it is ideal to sit close enough to overhear any conversation. As noted previously, two operators dining together provide cover for one operator to transmit information to the team while appearing to converse with the other operator.

If the operator inside the restaurant is expected to continue the follow when the target departs, he should order a meal that can be served quickly. This eliminates the possibility that he will have to depart before his meal arrives—thus presenting a very suspicious appearance to countersurveillance or other individuals. If the team is in position to establish a box outside the restaurant, there is no need for the operator to draw attention unnecessarily by asking to pay immediately. Any target that is surveillance conscious will be particularly sensitive to individuals who depart when he does.

Hotels and Motels

When the target enters a hotel or motel, an operator should follow and attempt to determine the room in which the target will reside. Conversation between the target and the receptionist is normally easily overheard. This information is critical in determining the most effective manner in which to cover the target while he resides at the location. This will also assist the team in determining the best location to establish an observation or listening post.

When the team is unable to determine the target's room initially, it is normally more secure to identify the location through foot surveillance rather than by calling the receptionist and attempting to elicit the information. Hotels are normally reluctant to divulge such information and may compromise the operation by informing the target that someone was interested in determining his room number. Regardless of whether the team establishes an observation or listening post in the hotel, selected operators should register for a hotel room if the target intends to stay more than one or two nights. This provides cover for action for the operators who are required to operate inside the hotel.

Post Offices

Post offices are another public location in which the surveillance team will normally be interested in observing the target's activities. A significant number of individuals involved in illegal or operational activity will use a post office box that is dissociated from their residence. By identifying the number of a post office box used by the target, the team will develop a significant lead to be exploited.

There is another situation involving the use of the postal system that may assist a surveillance. An individual who is involved in operational or illegal activity will rarely post mail from his residence or neighborhood when conducting such activity through the postal system. When a surveillance team suspects that a target is using the postal system for such purposes, it should prepare large manila envelopes with fictitious addresses. When the surveillance team observes the target place a letter in a mailbox, an operator will place a large envelope in the same mailbox after the target has departed.

This will help to isolate the letter for identification during an inspection of the mailbox contents. If not previously coordinated, the team should then attempt to gain authorization to search the mail for the target's letter. A sample of the target's handwriting will assist in conducting the search. Be advised that unauthorized tampering with the mail or bribing a postal worker to gain access to the target's letter is a federal offense. Once the target's letter is in hand, the team can either open and reseal it clandestinely or identify the contents by infrared film photography.

Financial Institutions

Other public locations that also warrant particular note are banks or other financial institutions. These locations can be indicative of the target's future activities. People normally visit the bank to do one of two things: to put money in, or take money out in the form of a withdrawal or a loan. When the surveillance team does not have the support of an agency that can obtain the target's bank records legally, it is often necessary for the surveillance team to develop information regarding the target's finances. This will be done primarily through surveillance of the target when he visits his financial institution. Without going into extensive detail, bank accounts are widely used as a secure means of transferring funds in support of illegal or operational activity.

Cash withdrawals or deposits can be indicative of future activities or an activity that has been conducted that reaped a payoff for the target. When the target enters a bank, the surveillance team should attempt to determine the purpose of the visit. In less crowded conditions, this can be fairly easy if an operator can engage a teller next to the one the target is using. Of course, the operator must establish a cover for action. This is a particularly important consideration since banks invariably employ security personnel or systems for the identification of suspicious individuals.

In crowded banks where the line is such that individuals must take the next teller who becomes available, it may be impossible for the operator to get close to the target. In such circumstances, it may be more effective for the operator to stay back in line so that he is in position to at least determine whether the target is making a deposit or a withdrawal. In any case, if the target makes a withdrawal, the team should be alerted and interpret this as an indicator that some type of significant activity will occur in the near future.

Travel Agencies

Travel agencies can also provide significant information regarding the target's future activities. The team needs to know if the target plans to take a trip in the near future. The fact that the target is taking a trip in the first place may provide information regarding his activities that had been previously unknown.

Another important aspect of the team being aware of a trip the target intends to take is that it gives them an opportunity to prepare.

When the surveillance team represents a government law

enforcement or intelligence agency, such previous knowledge provides time to work out the jurisdictional issues and coordinate support in the area the target intends to visit. Also, it is extremely difficult to continue an effective surveillance operation when the target travels unexpectedly to an airport and boards a plane. Such circumstances make it impossible for members of the team to be waiting at the destination ahead of the target. The only way to continue the surveillance at that point is to have operators take the flight with the target. Even if there are seats available for team members, when they land in an unfamiliar area they will have to continue the follow without standard support, to include not having organic surveillance vehicles for a vehicular follow. Surveillance inside bus stations, train stations, and airports will be addressed in Chapter 11.

Telephone Booths

One final note regarding surveillance in public locations and foot surveillance in general concerns the use of telephone booths by the target. When the target enters a telephone booth, once again the operator must determine if the information he anticipates developing is worth the risk involved. If the target enters a single booth, then the decision is academic, unless there is some unique type of cover that allows the operator to get close enough to overhear the conversation. Directional microphones are ideal for such situations, but the team will rarely have the forewarning necessary for this application.

When there are two booths together, an operator may be able to take up a position in another booth and overhear the target's conversation. If this is done, the operator must establish his cover for action by actually placing money in the phone and making a call. The operator must be aware that the target will be extremely suspicious of anyone's presence if he is having a conversation of an illegal or operational nature. Also, when there are multiple booths in a row, the normal individual would not select a booth directly next to an occupied one unless no other booths are available. By doing this, an operator would certainly draw suspicion from the target.

On many public phones there is a redial button for user convenience. A surveillance operator can use this redial button to determine where the target called, after the target has completed his call and departed the area. The operator must ensure that nobody else uses the phone after the target, or the redial button is of no use. The least secure method of using the redial is for the operator to place money in the phone and push the redial button, then by pretending to have gotten a wrong number or through some other ruse, attempt to elicit information regarding the individual on the other end as he answers.

The most secure method is to place a miniature tape recorder to the earpiece as the redial button is engaged. This will record the dial sequence, while giving the caller the opportunity to hang up the receiver before the call is actually connected. When he has an opportunity, the surveillance operator can slow the recording and match the button tones to those of a standard phone. If there is any question that the tones may be different, the operator can also make a quick recording of the button tones on the specific phone the target used after the redialed number has been recorded. Once the team deciphers the phone number, determining the location to which the phone is registered is basic investigative work.

COMBINED FOOT & VEHICULAR SURVEILLANCE

Combined foot and vehicular surveillance integrates the individual tactics of the two as a comprehensive operational practice. This is not to say that, given these tactics alone, a team can conduct a combined follow. There are many tactics unique to the transition from a vehicular surveillance to a foot surveillance, as well as the transition from foot to vehicular.

Normally, a surveillance will move initially from a vehicular follow to a foot follow, but this is not always the case. In any situation, the team must be prepared to make such transitions at any time. It is during this transition period, whether from foot or from vehicular, that the target is most difficult to command. These are situations in which the target has a distinct advantage over the surveillance team. Normally the target will be familiar with the terrain, thus facilitating a fluid transition. The surveillance team, on the other hand, must negotiate unfamiliar terrain while maintaining command of the target during this most vulnerable period.

TRANSITION FROM VEHICULAR TO FOOT SURVEILLANCE

The single most important objective of the transition from a vehicular to a foot surveillance is to get foot operators out of their vehicles and onto the ground quickly. To allow just a momentary period of lost command during the transition could result in the target disappearing—not to be seen again until (or unless) he returns to his vehicle. Recall that it is while on foot that the target can be expected to conduct his illegal or operational activities.

Not knowing when a transition will occur, the individual operators must be prepared for a transition at any time. This is why all of the operators on the team, to include the drivers, wear their body communications equipment at all times. They must have all such personal belongings as identification documents and sufficient money to cover any contingency. Since it is critical for foot operators to take to the ground immediately, there is no time to spare for an operator to get his personal effects in order. Once an operator exits the surveillance vehicle, there is no telling where the target may take him, and in any event it is very unlikely that he will return to the same surveillance vehicle when the transition back to vehicular surveillance occurs.

The first key to an effective transition from a vehicular surveillance to a foot follow is an accurate location of where the target has parked his vehicle. This is critical because the foot operators must be in a good position to begin the foot follow but should not exit their surveillance vehicles in sight of the target. With an accurate location of where the target has stopped, the navigators can examine the map to determine an appropriate location for their drivers to stop and let them out. It is important that at least one foot operator be dropped close enough to the target to establish initial command quickly. If this is not done, the foot follow may begin as a lost-command drill—which is not a good start.

As the navigator determines the best location to enter the follow, he will inform the team of his intentions and direct his driver to that location. Each surveillance vehicle informs the team of its intentions so as to avoid duplication of effort. As this is taking place, the navigator will quickly examine his map to establish a good general picture of the area. At a minimum, he should be oriented to the cardinal directions (north, south, east, west) prior to exiting the surveillance vehicle. The operator should also look for key landmarks to assist in orientation when on the ground. The last action taken prior to exiting the surveillance vehicle is to quickly identify the map location of the target vehicle to the driver. This is important because after the navigator exits the surveillance vehicle the driver is on his own, and there is much that the driver must do in support.

The location and manner in which the surveillance vehicle drops the foot operator should appear natural to any observers. In determining the most effective location to join the foot surveillance, the navigator may not be in position to maneuver to the exact location that the target went to ground. In any case, it is a poor security practice for multiple surveillance vehicles to drop foot operators at the same location or in the same location as the target vehicle. The navigator must assess the location of his surveillance vehicle in relation to the location of the target vehicle. By analyzing the terrain for possible routes of travel available to the target, he may identify a location to be dropped that is away from the target vehicle, yet in a strategically sound location to integrate into the follow.

In some cases the terrain may be suitable for foot operators to establish a floating box directly from their surveillance vehicles. Such a strategy may be particularly effective if the target goes unsighted initially. Rather than all of the operators attempting to catch up from behind, they may be able to position themselves in locations to cut the target off. Recall how the floating box can be collapsed to locate the target when unsighted. This concept can be applied immediately by the effective selection of drop locations for foot operators.

Figure 29 illustrates the concept of boxing drop locations. The target vehicle is parked in the lot at the bottom of the figure, where the target was last observed walking north on the adjacent road.

Surveillance vehicle Echo drops an operator to the south of the location of the target vehicle. This operator will travel north on that road in an attempt to establish initial command of the target. Surveillance vehicle Alpha drops an operator at the west end of the road which intersects the target's anticipated route of travel to the north. The operator begins checking for the target

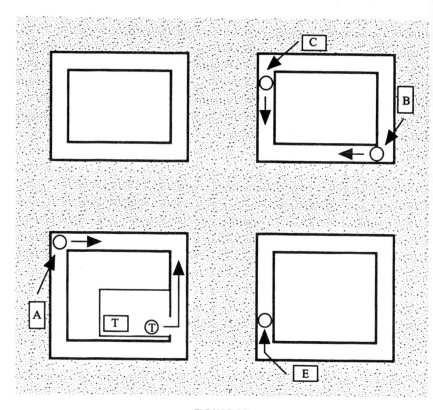

FIGURE 29

by traveling east on the road. Surveillance vehicle Bravo drops an operator on the east side of that same road. This operator checks west on that road for the target. Surveillance vehicle Charlie drops an operator farther to the north of the target's anticipated route of travel. This operator will travel south on that road checking for the target.

In this example, had a foot operator established initial command of the target, the floating box would have been established directly from the transition. As depicted in Figure 30, the operators on the east and west parallel routes will simply hold their positions until the command operator calls the target north through the paralleling intersection. At this point the paralleling operators will begin to travel north on their respective parallel routes.

The operator to the north of the follow will establish a con-

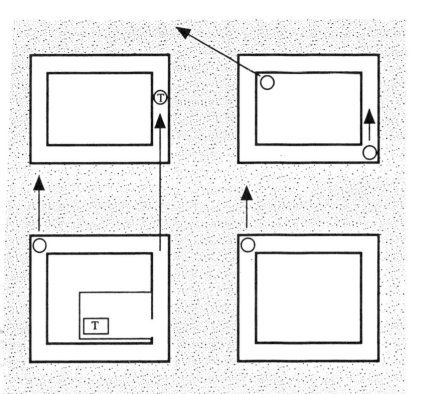

FIGURE 30

trol position and wait for the target and command operator to pass. When this occurs, the control operator will enter the follow as the backing operator. If the target were to turn east or west at the first intersection, the appropriate operator would establish a control position and wait for the target. In the event of a turn, the operator farther to the north would parallel the target's travel in the appropriate direction.

As a foot operator exits the surveillance vehicle, the driver will inform the team which operator (by name) is on the ground and, once again, what that operator's intentions are in support of the follow. Immediately after exiting, the foot operator will conduct a communications check with the surveillance vehicle. If communications are established, then the operator will continue on his mission. If, for any reason, there is a problem with the foot operator's communications equipment, he will immediately return to the surveillance vehicle until the problem has been corrected. An operator without functioning communications equipment is of no help to a team of operators with communications equipment. The operator would simply be wandering blindly, and may even interfere with the follow. If an operator in such a situation cannot correct the problem quickly, then the driver should exit the surveillance vehicle as a foot operator and let the operator with communications failure take over as the driver. Operators on the ground will transition to a foot surveillance follow as discussed in Chapters 8 and 9.

SURVEILLANCE VEHICLES IN SUPPORT OF FOOT SURVEILLANCE

When the target goes to ground, the priority for the surveillance vehicles is to support the foot operators in the follow. The only box position that must be established on the target vehicle is a trigger surveillance vehicle. This should be established immediately and remain throughout the foot operation. The trigger will give the team a degree of command, since it is likely that the target will eventually return to his vehicle. This is particularly important when the target is unsighted because the team will at least be assured that the target is out there somewhere and that they will be alerted when he returns to his vehicle. The other surveillance vehicles will maneuver around the operational area as necessary to support foot operators on the ground.

Communications

The most basic form of support that surveillance vehicles will provide the operators is communications. Recall that body communications equipment has a limited range. This may impair one foot operator's ability to hear another's transmissions. To overcome this shortcoming, surveillance vehicles will ensure that there is a communications link with each of the operators on the ground.

By doing this, the team will be able to communicate all important information to each member as necessary. The initial communications link between a surveillance vehicle and a foot operator is established when the operator exits the surveillance vehicle and conducts the initial communications check. At this point, that specific surveillance vehicle will support that specific operator. As the follow develops, it is neither efficient nor practical for that surveillance vehicle to remain dedicated to that operator for communications support. It is, however, that surveillance vehicle's responsibility to inform the team when it no longer has communications with the operator. When this occurs, other surveillance vehicles on the team will attempt to establish a communications link with the operator. If no other surveillance vehicle is able to do so, then the one that is closest to the operator's last known position will maneuver to establish communications. This process is a continuous one that applies to all of the operators on the ground.

In some types of terrain and atmospheric conditions, as few as one surveillance vehicle may be able to provide communications support to all the foot operators. Surveillance vehicles should maximize the advantage of elevation in providing communications support. Such locations as the top of a multilevel parking garage are ideal for communications links.

When an operator on the ground transmits pertinent information, the surveillance vehicle in support will retransmit this information to ensure that the entire team receives it. The supporting surveillance vehicles will also take notes based on the operators' transmissions.

Map Reading

Map reading is another important form of support that a surveillance vehicle will provide an operator. Regardless of how good a foot operator's sense of direction may be, even the best ones can get disoriented. With a surveillance vehicle in support, the map is only a communications link away. An operator will identify where he is on the ground by either a street intersection or a landmark that is reflected on the map. By providing this information to the supporting surveillance vehicle, the operator's location can be identified on the map. The surveillance vehicle will then direct the operator to the target's present location or to a location that the team needs that operator to cover. Surveillance vehicles will also provide map-reading support to operators directly involved in the follow. The surveillance vehicles can look ahead on the map and warn the operators of any obstacles or hazards they may be approaching.

Map-reading support is also key in orchestrating an effective floating box. Additionally, surveillance vehicles provide critical support to operators during a lost-command drill. Surveillance vehicles can direct the operators to check areas and locations that would not be apparent from an operator's vantage point. Surveillance vehicles can also ensure that an operator's efforts are not duplicating those of another. Furthermore, when the target is unsighted, surveillance vehicles can be employed to check the streets for the target, thus allowing foot operators to search inside public locations.

Transportation

Surveillance vehicles will support the operators by transporting them to locations that might take much longer for them to reach by foot. If for any reason an operator finds himself far from the location of the target, he can call a surveillance vehicle to pick him up and transport him closer to the target. This type of support is common to situations in which a lost-command drill has been ongoing for some time prior to the target being located. In such situations the foot team may be widely dispersed. Surveillance vehicles can be used to transport the operators for quick support of the follow.

Surveillance vehicles can also be used to transport operators ahead of the target to avoid traffic obstacles or in anticipation of hazards. For example, if the target is walking in the general direction of a subway station, it may be prudent to transport operators ahead to cover that hazard.

Transporting operators may also be necessary for security purposes. In open terrain where multiple operators can be observed to the rear of the target, operators can be transported ahead to avoid exposure. An excellent example of this is a follow across a long bridge. To commit multiple operators onto this type of channelized terrain would make them highly vulnerable to detection by either rear observation or a 180-degree turn. As the target is walking across such a feature, surveillance vehicles can transport operators ahead via a parallel bridge to avoid sending more than one operator across the bridge behind the target.

Surveillance vehicles will also provide support to an operator who has been exposed to the target. It will normally be necessary for that operator to exchange duties with the driver of a surveillance vehicle, sending the driver out as a foot operator. In other circumstances, the surveillance vehicle will be needed to bring the operator a change of clothes and a disguise kit.

SHUTTING DOWN A SURVEILLANCE VEHICLE

In some circumstances it may be necessary to park and leave surveillance vehicles unmanned in order to increase the number of foot operators. When this is done, it is important for the operator of the parked vehicle to inform the team of the vehicle's exact location.

This is necessary because that operator may not be the one to return to the surveillance vehicle. If, for instance, the target boards a train and that operator is the one in position to board behind the target, he should not allow the target to escape because he is the only one who knows the location of, and has the keys to, a surveillance vehicle. If copies of all of the surveillance vehicle keys are not maintained in each of the vehicles, then the operator must place the keys in a predetermined location on the vehicle before departing. This will allow any operator to man the surveillance vehicle immediately whenever necessary.

Putting keys under the wheel well is common, but this is not very secure. If the operator can place the keys up the tail pipe of the surveillance vehicle without being observed by anyone, they will certainly be there when an operator goes to man that surveillance vehicle.

ESTABLISHING THE BOX

The last priority of a combined foot and vehicular surveillance when the target is on the ground is to establish a box on the target vehicle. Other than the trigger vehicle, the priority for the team's surveillance vehicles is to support the foot operators. If the foot operators are receiving sufficient support and there are surveillance vehicles remaining, those vehicles will establish box positions around the target vehicle. It is likely that there will not be enough surveillance vehicles available to establish a complete box. Available surveillance vehicles will establish their positions based on the prioritization of the most likely routes the target will travel when departing by vehicle. When the target is unsighted, any surveillance vehicles not providing critical support to foot operators should establish box positions. This is advisable because the target could return to his vehicle at any time without forewarning.

TRANSITION FROM FOOT TO VEHICULAR SURVEILLANCE

When the target indicates that he intends to return to his vehicle, the transition from foot to vehicular surveillance will begin. Normally, as the target walks in the general direction of his vehicle, he will bring the foot operators close enough to the target vehicle for the surveillance vehicles to begin establishing a vehicular box while still providing communications support. When this point is reached, the surveillance vehicles will establish a surveillance box using the standard boxing principles.

If surveillance vehicles can pick up operators on their way to a box position without degrading their ability to do so, then this will be done. It must be understood, however, that at this point, establishing the surveillance vehicle box to ensure a pickup of the target vehicle takes priority over picking up operators. Additionally, it serves little purpose for a surveillance vehicle to go to any additional effort to pick up the operator that was in the surveillance vehicle originally. If an operator is fortunate enough to be picked up prior to the vehicular follow beginning, he will be satisfied with whichever surveillance vehicle collects him.

As the target enters his vehicle and departs, the team will conduct a pickup and vehicular follow just like any other. In such situations, however, drivers will likely be conducting the vehicular follow without a navigator. It takes a high degree of expertise to read the map and make radio calls while driving and observing the target, but a skilled team can execute such a follow with little additional difficulty.

Unless the team requires all its surveillance vehicles to be involved in the initial follow, one or two surveillance vehicles will remain behind to pick up any remaining foot operators. Normally the surveillance vehicle that acted as trigger in the box will be one of those surveillance vehicles, if not the only one. This surveillance vehicle will coordinate rendezvous locations with each of the operators and pick them up as expeditiously as possible. As with the dropoff, the pickup should be in a logical location to avoid drawing undue attention. This is particularly applicable if the target is still in the area. After the follow has progressed and the target is stabilized in another location, the operators will be transported to any surveillance vehicles without navigators.

If all the surveillance vehicles are required for the vehicular follow, remaining foot operators will allow some time for the follow to progress and then at some point telephone one of the surveillance vehicles—if this capability exists. If there are no phones in the surveillance vehicles, then the team should have a control base established for the operators to call.

If this capability exists, the surveillance vehicles can call the base with the target's location when he is somewhat stabilized. Either from a surveillance vehicle phone or the base phone, the operators can get the location of the surveillance vehicles and the target. With this information, the operators will take public transportation to an appropriate location for a rendezvous with a surveillance vehicle.

If the vehicular team has neither the capability to be contacted in its surveillance vehicles or through a control base, then the operators will rendezvous at a predetermined location. When the situation allows, the team will dispatch a surveillance vehicle to pick up the operators at that location.

PUBLIC

TRANSPORTATION

SURVEILLANCE

Without a doubt, public transportation is the most difficult challenge to a surveillance team. This is the most effective mode of transportation for a target who is practicing antisurveillance. Probably, the biggest disadvantage in the surveillance of a target who uses public transportation is that the team can become widely dispersed in a short period of time. Particularly when operating against a target who uses mass transit, such as the subway, the team will experience significant communications problems as well.

As with all types of surveillance, preparation is critical to the success of a surveillance against a target using public transportation. The public transportation systems of most cities follow some type of logical routing. By understanding the systemic basis to a city's transportation system, the team can adapt and react better to the target's travels.

Schedules and route maps of the public transportation system are essential. When a target enters a bus or subway train, it is necessary for the team to identify the route of that particular mode of transportation and the possible locations along that route to which the target can travel. All operators should have sufficient money in the correct form of change to make a quick and natural transition to any mode of public transportation when the circumstances of the surveillance dictate.

SURVEILLANCE OF TAXICABS

The surveillance of a taxi is the easiest form of surveillance involving public transportation. It is generally the same as the surveillance of any other vehicle. When the target enters a taxi, it is critical that the command vehicle or operator inform the team of the taxi's appearance. A full description of the taxi should include the license number and any logo that may be displayed on the exterior.

In some regions, such as Europe, it can be more difficult to follow a taxi because they use standard vehicles, and they are all in perfect condition. This makes it difficult to distinguish one taxi from another, particularly in locations with high concentrations of taxis, such as airports or bus stations. In the United States, however, individual taxis are normally unique enough to pose no significant identification problem to the team. If a telephone number is displayed on the taxi, this should be recorded for later use if necessary.

One primary concern when following a taxi is that it is driven by a "professional" driver. This implies that the driver maneuvers through and observes surrounding traffic as a way of life. The taxi driver will be intimately familiar with the terrain, whereas the surveillance team likely will not be. This may result in the taxi outmaneuvering the team, not intentionally but because of standard driver efficiency. Another concern in this respect is that the taxi driver will be more observant of surrounding traffic than would be the standard soft target. This raises the possibility that the taxi driver may detect surveillance vehicles and tip the target to any suspicious activity. A taxi driver's motivation in doing this is that such a tip may result in a reciprocal monetary tip from the target.

As the surveillance team members conduct the follow of a taxi, they must constantly read ahead on the map to anticipate possible hazards. People do not take taxis for joyrides; they take them with a specific destination in mind. If the team members can look ahead to anticipate possible destinations, they may place themselves in a better position to transition to a foot follow when the target exits the taxi. When the target exits the taxi, surveillance vehicles will drop off foot operators immediately to begin the foot follow, as discussed in the previous chapter.

When a surveillance team does not have surveillance vehicle support to conduct a follow of a taxi, virtually the only option is for an operator to enter another taxi to follow the target. The operator should explain to the taxi driver that he wants him to follow a friend in the other taxi. The operator should further qualify this by saying that he does not want his friend to know that he is being followed because he wants to surprise him. This may persuade the taxi driver to be more discreet in his follow, but a seasoned taxi driver may not be taken in by this ploy.

Regardless of the driver's reaction, the offer of monetary compensation for his cooperation will likely ensure compliance. This can be a very risky tactic, however, if the driver does not drive with the utmost discretion.

If the target is lost while traveling by taxi, the number and company of the taxi are exploitable leads in determining the target's destination. Most taxi drivers must maintain a log of times and passenger destinations to provide their company at the end of each day. When all other options of locating the target have been expended, the team can contact the taxi company and attempt to elicit the destination of that particular taxi at the time when the target was the passenger. As always, money is an effective elicitation technique when other methods fail. The company should not be contacted while there is a possibility that the target is still in the taxi because the taxi may be contacted by the company.

SURVEILLANCE OF BUSES

The surveillance of a target who travels by bus requires an understanding of some unique principles. Once again, as the target enters a bus, it is important for the team to have a full description. Buses for city transportation will bear an identification number that indicates its specified route. The team should have maps with the city bus routes illustrated on them. By matching the bus number with the route on the map, the team can identify where the bus is going and at which locations it will stop.

The team should always attempt to have an operator on the bus with the target for positive command. The ideal situation is to observe the target at a bus stop and transport an operator to the bus stop before the target's own. This enables the operator to board the bus before the target does, making his presence very inconspicuous.

In this case, the operator should select a seat as far to the rear of the bus as possible. If an operator is unable to enter the bus at a stop prior to the target's, a surveillance vehicle will transport an operator ahead to another stop on the bus' route. The operator will then enter at a different stop than did the target, making his presence less suspicious.

If the bus has more than one entrance, the operator should enter by the one closest to the rear. This will minimize the possibility that the operator will have to walk past the target on the way to the rear or have to sit to the front of the target. Operators should be familiar with the method of payment because this may also determine which entrance to use. The operator will attempt to sit to the rear of the target, so that he can observe the target in a natural manner. If the target has specifically selected to sit at the very rear of the bus, the operator should immediately become sensitive to the possibility of surveillance detection on the part of the target.

An operator on a bus with the target will have difficulty communicating with the team except through the voiceless method. This is not a significant factor because the only critical information the operator will likely have to transmit to the team is when the target is intending to exit the bus or a personal meeting between the target and another individual. The standard series of transmissions on a bus is discussed below. Once again, Drake is the foot operator on the bus with the target. Drake will initiate the transmission when he is seated and in command of the target.

> *Drake:* Multiple clicks or steady rush of static
> *Interrogator:* Is that Drake?
> *Drake:* Two clicks (affirmative response)
> *Interrogator:* Drake, are you in command?
> *Drake:* Two clicks (affirmative response)

Interrogator: Drake, is the target in contact?
Drake: No clicks (possible negative response)
Interrogator: Drake, is the target not in contact?
Drake: Two clicks (affirmative response)
Interrogator: Drake, do you have anything else to tell me?
Drake: No clicks (possible negative response)
Interrogator: Drake, do you not have anything else to tell me?
Drake: Two clicks (affirmative response)

At this point the interrogation is complete until it is initiated once again by the operator on the bus. Unless the target subsequently comes into contact with another individual, the next transmission from the operator on the bus should be to alert the team that the target is intending to exit. When the operator gives the next series of clicks, the interrogator should immediately ask the operator if the target is intending to exit the bus. If the interrogator gets a negative response, he should ask if the target is in contact.

While the operator is on the bus with the target, the team should provide pertinent information to that operator. As the bus is approaching the next-to-last stop on the route, the team should direct the operator to exit at that stop if the target does not. This is done because the team knows that the target will exit at either of these stops, and it will allow the operator to exit at a different stop than the target, thus drawing less suspicion. If the target does not exit at either of the stops, then the team should strongly suspect surveillance detection or antisurveillance on the part of the target. If the target had intended to travel to a stop that occurred prior to his entering the bus, then it would have been more logical for him to have taken a bus in the opposite direction.

The frequent stops of a bus make a standard vehicular follow risky. This presents little difficulty, however, since the bus' route of travel is known. Rather than following from the rear, which is standard for most vehicular follows, the surveillance of a bus concentrates on the forward positioning of vehicles in anticipation of the transition to a foot follow. Because of the slow rate of travel of most buses and the multiple stops along the route, the team should have adequate time to maneuver ahead in anticipation of the target's eventual exit.

Separate surveillance vehicles should maneuver ahead of the

bus to have at least one or two operators available to establish a foot follow at each stop. During this process, drawing the attention of an observant bus driver is more likely than drawing the target's attention. On a long bus route, the chances of the same surveillance vehicle having to pass the bus a number of times is likely. Paralleling routes should be used to minimize exposure when possible.

While the target is on the bus, the team must look ahead to anticipate possible hazards. Primary hazards consist of locations where the bus' route intersects the route of another form of public transportation. Bus stops in the vicinity of a subway station are of particular concern. At such locations, the team will probably choose to have more foot operators waiting in anticipation of a foot follow than would be waiting at a normal stop along the route. This is necessary because the target can be underground and on a subway in a very short period of time.

When the team is unable to get an operator on the bus, or the operator does not have a communications capability, surveillance vehicles must be positioned at each stop to observe the people who exit. This is a disadvantage in that it requires vehicles to spend more time at each stop than would be necessary if there were an operator on the bus to inform the team when the target exits. It is also a disadvantage in that there is far less reaction time for the vehicles positioned at different locations to maneuver and support the foot follow when the target does exit. This should rarely be necessary, however, because unless the team strongly suspects surveillance detection by the target, there is little reason not to place an operator on the bus. An exception to this is when the bus has very few additional passengers for cover. In this case, there will be few enough passengers exiting at each stop to see clearly when the target exits. Another exception, of course, is when operators do not have body communications equipment. An operator without communications equipment would only enter a bus with the target when the objectives of the operation dictate that the target be observed at this point.

When the target exits the bus, the team will switch to a standard foot surveillance. Surveillance vehicles that are not at the location will transport operators to support the follow. Actions taken during the surveillance of a target inside a bus terminal are similar to those employed in a train station or airport. These will be discussed in subsequent sections.

If the target is lost during the transition from vehicular to foot surveillance and the lost-command drill meets with negative results, the team should stake out the bus stop at which the target departed. This concept applies unless there is credible information to indicate the target's destination. Even when this is the case, it is prudent to employ a trigger surveillance vehicle or operator to observe the bus stop.

SURVEILLANCE ON MASS TRANSIT

Surveillance on mass transit systems such as subways and metros is most difficult. The team is certain to experience communications difficulties because the target is underground. Even operators conducting the follow inside a subway station may experience communications difficulties because of interference from the other electrical signals contained in the confined area. The team outside the subway station will also become widely dispersed, impeding the transition from subway follow to foot follow. A surveillance team must be well trained and coordinated in order to execute the subway surveillance effectively.

A follow on a subway should begin as the team initially anticipates that the target intends to enter a subway station. The minimum number of operators to go into the subway station with the target will be four. This number will be increased depending on the number of operators necessary to command the target inside the subway station. Additionally, if the target is expected to take subway connections between more than one train, the number of foot operators should be increased proportionately. A team without body communications equipment will need to concentrate more operators inside the station to maintain the integrity of the follow.

Because of the underground status of most subway stations, the team should anticipate that radio communications to outside surveillance vehicles and operators will be ineffective while operating within. Foot operators, however, should be able to communicate with each other while operating within the station. For this reason, it will be necessary to dedicate a foot operator to relay communications.

One of the at least four operators who enters the subway station behind the target will designate himself as a relay. This operator will position himself in a location where he can hear the transmissions of the command operator and quickly relay the information to the team outside. One method of doing this is to keep an open telephone line to one of the surveillance vehicles while monitoring the other operators' transmissions.

If this option is not available, the relay operator must position himself so that he can quickly move aboveground when there is critical information to relay. This may require that the operator make many trips up and down to maintain the relay. Two operators may be necessary to relay in tandem in stations that require a lengthy transition aboveground.

Foot operators will inform the team as they enter the subway station so that the reason for lost communications contact is understood. While one of the operators is establishing himself as the relay, the other operators will execute a foot follow. The first priority is to determine the type of ticket the target purchases because this provides some indication of the target's extent of travel.

The next information the operators should provide the team is the subway line that the target moves to. The team will have subway schedules in the surveillance vehicles if they are prepared. With this information they can determine the route the target intends to travel and begin planning accordingly. If the surveillance vehicles do not have subway schedules, the foot operators must relay this information as well.

When the target enters a subway train, the operators will relay the information to the team and enter the train behind the target. One operator will enter the same compartment of the train as the target to establish command during the ride. This operator will attempt to position himself behind and out of the target's view. The other operators will enter adjoining compartments while remaining out of the target's sight. At least two of the operators will sit together in a seat near as few people as possible. One of these two operators will interrogate the command operator while appearing to converse with the other operator.

The interrogation process will consist of the same questions asked during the bus follow. As the command operator informs the other operators that the target is intending to exit the train, they too will prepare to exit and conduct a foot follow. If the command operator can also exit the train without alerting the target, he will do so. This operator, however, will not join in the follow. He will move quickly to contact the team and provide information regarding the target's location.

If telephone contact is not possible, then he will move above-ground and attempt to contact the team by radio. If the team has anticipated the target's possible actions correctly, a surveillance vehicle may be in the area. When contact is established, that operator will act as the relay for the operators conducting the follow. If the command operator is unable to depart the train because of security reasons, then one of the other operators will attempt to contact the team.

When the target exits one subway train and moves to catch another, the operators should transmit this information to the operator who has established himself as a relay. The relay will attempt to contact team members outside the station to provide the information. The other operators will follow the target onto the next train and position themselves as previously discussed. If the surveillance vehicles reach the station in a timely manner, additional operators or replacements will enter the station to join the follow.

SURVEILLANCE ON TRAINS

The surveillance of a target traveling by train is very similar to the subway surveillance. The team will establish a relay operator to provide the team outside the station with pertinent information. Many train stations facilitate adequate outside communications, negating the need for a relay.

Purchasing a ticket for a train is normally a more formal process than for the subway. If the target does not already have his ticket, he will have to go to a ticket window and purchase one. The operators inside the train station must make every effort to determine the target's destination as soon as possible. To develop this information, an operator must be close enough to overhear the conversation between the target and the ticket window attendant. The operator should also attempt to ascertain the train compartment and seat that the target is issued.

Once the surveillance team receives information regarding the target's destination, it can determine if it is feasible to send vehicles ahead to that location. If the team intends to continue the follow at the destination, the members should consider sending the surveillance vehicles. Even if the surveillance vehicles cannot reach the destination prior to the train, they will still be better late than never. If the team simply intends to turn the follow over to another investigative agency at the destination, then surveillance vehicles will be unnecessary.

When sending the surveillance vehicles, at least one vehicle should remain at the train station in case the target does not take the anticipated train. In this event, the stay-behind surveillance vehicle can inform the other surveillance vehicles to move to another destination or return to the original station. When the vehicles are sent to the destination, the operators taking the train will be informed of when vehicle support is expected to arrive. When it is not feasible to send vehicles, but the surveillance is to continue at the destination, portable vehicle surveillance communications kits configured in suitcases can be carried aboard by operators.

Whether or not surveillance vehicles are sent ahead will have a significant impact on the number of operators who must travel on the train with the target. If the team intends to continue the follow at the destination without vehicle support, then they should place as many operators on the train as possible. The operators must ensure that there is sufficient time to purchase tickets for themselves. As with the subway follow, the minimum number of operators on the train should be three. The team must also determine if the objectives of the operation warrant having an operator close to the target for the duration of the train ride. In doing this, the command operator will certainly be compromised and of no further use at the destination. This is an excellent example of a situation in which an operator can use a disguise in advance to protect his true appearance.

When the team selects to have an operator close enough to the target to observe him during the trip, two other operators will be positioned together to conduct the interrogation as explained in the subway follow.

On train rides of long duration, the team will probably choose to turn off their radios to conserve battery life. An operator who is positioned in the same compartment or relatively close to the target will probably do this for security reasons. When there is a command operator, the team will turn on their radios at each stop in case the command operator informs them that the target is exiting prematurely.

When there is not a command operator while the train is traveling, or when radios have been turned off, the operators should attempt to position themselves in locations where they will be able to see if the target moves to the exit at a stop. If this is not possible, an operator must position himself to observe outside the train at each stop to ensure that the target does not exit prematurely.

When the train reaches the destination, one operator will exit the train immediately and take up a discreet trigger position to observe the target as he exits the train. If other operators can exit the train and position themselves ahead in control positions, they should do so. If they cannot do this without ensuring that the target will not see them, they should stay on the train until the target has exited and walked past their locations. At least one operator should remain on the train until after the target has exited.

When there is a command operator on the train, that operator should be the one to remain on the train until after the target has exited. If surveillance vehicles reach the train station prior to the target's train, they will establish an operator as a relay.

If the surveillance vehicles have not reached the train station but are expected, an operator from the train follow will attempt to contact the surveillance vehicles by whatever means available. As the target exits the train the foot surveillance team will conduct a pickup and foot follow. The team must be prepared to conduct a taxi follow immediately upon exiting the train station. When surveillance vehicles are not present in support and the situation allows, vehicles should be rented.

SURVEILLANCE ON AIRPLANES

The surveillance of a target on an airplane usually raises unique difficulties. Unless the team has prior knowledge of the flight, there will be no possibility of surveillance vehicle support at the destination unless another investigative agency can be contacted for support.

If the team does have prior knowledge of the flight, they can send operators ahead on an earlier flight to coordinate for surveillance vehicles and the pickup at the destination. In such cases, it will normally be necessary to have only one operator on the plane with the target.

The exceptions to this are flights that have lengthy layovers or when the target must change flights at an intermediate destination. Such situations may provide the target time to conduct illegal or operational activity that the team must attempt to observe. Intermediate airports along the target's flight schedule, which are not necessarily associated with his final destination, are common locations for clandestine meetings.

In many cases, the team will have no indication that the target intends to travel by air until they observe him depart his residence with a suitcase and travel to the airport. In these circumstances the same principles discussed in the train follow of determining the target's destination as early as possible apply. When the team members determine where the target intends to fly, they will then decide whether it is feasible to continue the follow. If the follow is necessary, the team must place sufficient operators on the plane to conduct an effective follow at the destination.

An immediate concern when intending to conduct a surveillance operation on an airplane is the security practices that are common to all airports. The continued carrying of firearms is rarely worth the difficulties involved. Security scanners will detect the body communications equipment whether worn or enclosed in carry-on baggage. When used in official status, the equipment can be cleared if done securely, but even the most thorough precautions will raise the profile of the surveillance operators. As a common practice the pilot and crew will be informed of the presence of undercover agents on the plane. Communications equipment should be checked through in regular baggage, although this causes transition difficulties at the destination. A standard radio antenna should also be included to provide a vehicular communications capability at the destination. When possible, portable vehicle surveillance communications kits configured in suitcases can be checked through as baggage for a vehicular surveillance capability at the destination.

If the team is able to determine the target's seat on the plane, they should purchase tickets in locations that will minimize the possibility of being seen by the target while on the flight. The seats selected should be closer to the nose of the plane than the target's seat if possible. If this is accomplished the operators will board the plane after the target to avoid walking by him when they take their seats. When the objectives of the operation dictate that an operator observe the target while on the plane, that operator should attempt to select a seat behind the target. This operator will make every effort to board the plane ahead of the target.

Other members of the team who are not on the plane can sometimes be called from the plane. Many airplanes have telephones that can be used with a calling card. Operators on the plane can call ahead to get information regarding the pickup preparation at the destination or to arrange for rental vehicles at the destination.

When the plane lands, the team members in front of the target on the plane will exit as early as possible and establish box positions in the airport. If the target checked his baggage through, he will eventually go to the baggage claims area. If this is the case, then it will only require one or two operators to command the target to the baggage claims area. The delay involved in the target waiting for his baggage should allow operators time to rent vehicles. When the number of operators is limited, the acquisition of vehicles should take priority over following the target from the gate to the baggage claims area.

Operators observing the target should be mindful that if he makes a telephone call, then there is a possibility he will be picked up by an associate. If an operator can overhear such a conversation, the information will prove critical to the success of the vehicular pickup. If this information is not available, then the operators of rented vehicles should begin to identify control box position locations from taxi stands and public pickup areas. Body communications equipment checked through in baggage can be used with a standard radio antenna for a communications capability in rented vehicles.

PROGRESSIVE SURVEILLANCE

Progressive surveillance is the phased coverage of a target to determine specific travel patterns or specific routes of travel. Progressive operations are the most secure method of surveillance because the surveillance team's degree of exposure to the target is limited. It is the method commonly employed by terrorists and assassins because of their extreme security requirements.

Despite this use by the criminal element, progressive surveillance is applicable for any surveillance team under various circumstances. Progressive surveillance operations are also conducted when limited resources restrict the surveillance team from the practice of extended foot, vehicular, or combined operations. The primary resource constraints are limited personnel or the lack of communications equipment.

Progressive surveillance is conducted through the use of mobile surveillance, fixed surveillance, or a combination of the two. The objective of a progressive operation is to determine the route or routes of travel a target takes from a common point of origin. If the objective is to determine the route the target takes to work, then the operation will begin at his residence. If the objective is to determine where the target goes after work, the operation will begin at the workplace. The objective of the operation may be further narrowed by attempting to determine the target's route of travel only on specific days when illegal or operational activity is expected to occur.

The basic concept of the progressive surveillance is to follow the target or observe his travel from a point of origin. The target is observed as he travels from the point of origin until he reaches a particular location, where the surveillance is terminated. The next phase of the operation will be based from the location where the previous one was terminated. At this point, the target will be observed as he travels farther along the route to another location, at which point the operation is again terminated. The next phase of the operation will be based again from the location where the previous one was terminated. This practice will continue until the objective of the operation is satisfied.

This method of surveillance is not as simple as it may appear. To start with, it takes a great deal of patience. No target will progress through a standard succession of routes everyday. Many days will be expended observing the target take a route that's not consistent with the objective of the operation. Other days will be expended manning a location farther along the specified route at which the target never appears.

A concept common to both mobile and fixed progressive surveillance operations is the use of *decision points*. These are locations that provide the target an option to turn or continue straight. The most common decision points are street intersections. Each phase of the progressive surveillance will normally be centered on determining the target's direction of travel from the decision point at which the surveillance will be terminated. The next phase of the operation will then be centered on determining the target's direction of travel from a decision point along the route of travel, based from the origin of the previous phase's terminating decision point.

Decision points do not necessarily have to be established at each possible successive point along the anticipated route of travel. In fact, to narrow the scope of each phase of an operation to one-block iterations of decision points will result in an unnecessarily lengthy operation. In determining the appropriate decision points to use, the team will assess the target's primary or most logical routes of travel available. Key intersections along these routes will be selected as decision points.

MOBILE PROGRESSIVE SURVEILLANCE OPERATIONS

The principles of mobile progressive surveillance are similar for both foot and vehicular operations. Whether the team uses foot or vehicular surveillance is dictated by the mode of travel employed by the target. In preparation for the mobile progressive operation, the team will conduct a recon of possible routes that the target may travel along from the designated point of origin.

Based on this examination, the team will determine likely decision points to which the target may be expected to travel. Prior to the beginning of the operation, the team will determine one decision point at which the initial phase will be terminated along each possible route of travel from the point of origin. These points are referred to as *terminating decision points*. It is necessary to identify a terminating decision point along each possible route because it will not yet have been established which route the target will take.

When conducting a mobile progressive surveillance, the team must establish a stakeout box at the point of origin. The box will be as elaborate or simple as necessary depending on the objective and method of the operation. The pickup of the target will be executed, and the follow will continue to the designated terminating decision point along the target's route of travel. The direction of the target's travel from that decision point will be noted and the surveillance terminated. If the target turns off prior to reaching the terminating decision point, that phase of the operation will be terminated at that location.

The next phase of the operation will be planned with the location of the unanticipated turn as the previous phase's terminating decision point. Although all subsequent examples will assume that the target reaches a designated terminating decision point, this factor always applies.

As the operation progresses, the team will continually assess the route being developed to determine the appropriate decision point

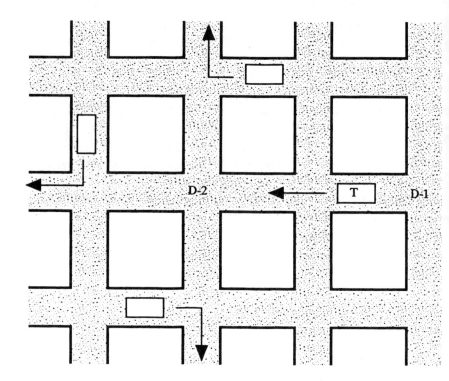

FIGURE 31

for the beginning of the next phase of the operation. The next phase's stakeout box will be established at the next appropriate decision point along the route on which the target traveled after passing through the previous phase's terminating decision point.

This decision point is referred to as the *base decision point*. The stakeout is established at a decision point farther along the established route because it is assumed that, if the target travels in the same direction, he will continue to the next designated decision point. This allows the team to continue the progressive surveillance operation at least one decision point farther in each phase. Once again, terminating decision points for the current phase will be designated for each possible route the target may travel along from the base decision point.

Figure 31 depicts the target's direction of travel after passing through the previous phase's terminating decision point (D-1) and the stakeout box established to cover all possible routes of travel from the current phase's base decision point (D-2). Although not depicted in the figure, each route from point D-2 will have an established terminating decision point.

The mobile operation will continue in this manner until the target fails to reach a base decision point. Provided that the target has been traveling in a standard pattern, the team will assume that the target's destination is located between the base decision point and the previous phase's terminating decision point, or that the target is taking a route that is available prior to the base decision point. When this occurs, the team will use the previous phase's terminating decision point as the next phase's base decision point. The final phase of the operation will consist of a pickup and follow from the base decision point to the destination. If the target takes a turn rather than traveling to a destination, the next phase of the operation will be planned based on the location of that turn as the terminating decision point.

A simpler method of the mobile progressive operation consists of the team establishing the base decision for each successive phase at the previous phase's terminating decision point. This method requires more individual phases but allows for a redundancy in coverage, which has its advantages. One advantage is that the team can be (fairly) certain of which direction the target will travel from the stakeout location. This assists in establishing more secure box positions for the stakeout. Additionally, this method only requires that the team designate one terminating decision point for each phase rather than one for each possible route of travel. This allows for the operation to be conducted by as few as one operator or one surveillance vehicle. One final advantage to this method is that the team does not have to backtrack from decision points when the target does not reach the base decision point, as is the case with the previous method discussed.

FIXED PROGRESSIVE SURVEILLANCE OPERATIONS

The fixed progressive surveillance operation is composed of static observation points established at decision points. This may consist of only one observation point or multiple points along an anticipated route of travel. The method used will normally depend on the assets available. The use of multiple points will decrease the length of the operation proportionately. Remote monitoring, mobile surveillance systems, and tactical observation posts are secure alternatives to establishing fixed positions with foot operators or surveillance vehicles.

The team will begin its preparation in a similar manner to that of the mobile progressive operation. The team will conduct a recon of possible routes that the target may travel along from the designated point of origin. Based on this examination, the team will determine likely decision points to which the target may be expected to travel. Prior to the beginning of the operation, the team will determine one terminating decision point along each possible route of travel from the point of origin. If there are sufficient operators to man a fixed position at a terminating decision point along each possible route from the point of origin, it is unnecessary to establish a fixed position at the point of origin. If there are not enough operators to do this, then the first priority for a fixed position is at the point of origin. Any additional operators will establish positions at designated terminating decision points along the most likely routes of travel.

The initial phase of the fixed progressive surveillance consists of determining which direction the target travels from the point of origin. If the team is able to man decision points on each of the possible routes of travel, this phase will also determine which direction the target travels from the first terminating decision point. The next phase of the operation will be based from the next decision point along the route on which the target traveled after passing through the previous phase's terminating decision point. Once again, if the team has sufficient operators to cover decision points along each possible route of travel from the base decision point; this should be done. If the team has a limited number of operators, a fixed position will be established at the base decision point. Any additional operators will establish positions at terminating decision points along the most likely routes of travel.

Figure 32 depicts the positioning of surveillance operators to observe the target's possible directions of travel after passing through the current phase's base decision point (D).

The target's anticipated direction of approach as depicted in the

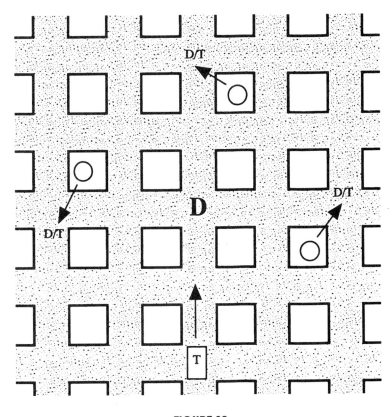

FIGURE 32

figure is based on his direction of travel after passing through the previous phase's terminating decision point. Since there is a sufficient number of operators to cover a terminating decision point (D/T) on each of the possible routes, a fixed position is not necessary at the base decision point (D). As the target travels through one of the terminating decision points, the appropriate operator will observe and note the target's route of travel away from the point. The next phase of the operation will be planned around a base decision point along the newly established route of travel.

In this example, if there were a sufficient number of operators to establish a fixed position at the base decision point (D) as well, this could provide valuable information in the event that the target fails to reach a terminating decision point. By identifying the target's direction of travel from the base decision point (D), the team would at least be aware of which direction the target traveled after passing through that point. This would indicate that the target reached a destination or turned before reaching the terminating decision point along that route.

The operation will continue in this manner until the target fails to reach a terminating decision point. When this occurs, the next phase of the operation will require that the team backtrack its positioning to determine the target's destination or another route by which the target is traveling. When this occurs, the team must limit the operation to successive decision points along the anticipated route of travel. The previous phase's terminating decision point will be established as the next phase's base decision point.

Any number of fixed positions can be established at successive decision points along the anticipated route of travel to maximize the probability of success. At this point in the operation, it is advantageous to integrate a mobile follow from the base decision point to the target's destination. This spares the team from timely backtracking and guesswork.

COMBINED FIXED AND MOBILE
PROGRESSIVE SURVEILLANCE OPERATIONS

Another method of progressive surveillance involves the integration of mobile and fixed surveillance. This is particularly effective after the team has conducted a number of mobile phases. By establishing fixed positions at decision points prior to the point at which the mobile operation is anticipated, the team can determine where the target deviates from the route if he does not reach the base decision point. This allows the team to determine variations in the target's pattern for the planning of future phases.

13

NIGHT SURVEILLANCE OPERATIONS

Historically, darkness has drawn espionage agents, terrorists, and the criminal element alike. It is the cover of darkness that gives such adversaries a sense of security when practicing their tradecraft. Consequently, much of the operational or illegal activity employed by a surveillance team will occur under the cover of night.

Nighttime surveillance is significantly different from that of daytime. The basic tactics remain the same, but there are many additional considerations imposed by darkness. The very nature of night surveillance dictates that the operators concentrate on more technically intricate tactical applications. These technical aspects unique to night surveillance will be the emphasis of this chapter.

NIGHT SURVEILLANCE EQUIPMENT

Night surveillance requires additional equipment, the proper application of which can turn the disadvantages of darkness in favor of the surveillance team. For this reason, the primary prerequisite for operators involved in night operations is a practical knowledge of these equipment peculiarities.

Flashlight

A flashlight is the most basic equipment requirement for night surveillance. The night not only brings darkness to the surveillance vehicle's surroundings but also to its interior. Obviously, a surveillance vehicle cannot conduct a follow with its interior light on and expect to remain inconspicuous. Without a flashlight, the navigator is helpless. For team members to rely on maps they must be able to read them. The flashlights should be palm-size models and should be equipped with color-shaded lenses because the colors on many maps do not show under the light of a standard white beam. Shaded lights also limit the amount of light that can be seen from outside the surveillance vehicle.

Night Vision Devices

Night vision devices (NVDs) provide the greatest advantage that the surveillance team will have over the target at night. They provide a significant stand-off-distance capability for enhanced security. There are two primary types of NVDs: *passive* and *active*. Passive devices magnify existing illumination for enhanced vision. Active devices generate their own light source through an infrared beam. Passive devices require some degree of existing illumination from such sources as the stars, moon, or streetlights, whereas active devices are capable of observation in total darkness.

Infrared NVDs with spot illuminators or long-range zoom laser illuminators provide further enhancement to an active capability. Active devices can also provide visibility through fog, smoke, and haze. A primary drawback to infrared is that in creating its own light source it emits a red beam. This beam is almost undetectable, but a dull red light appears when shone directly into the eyes of an individual. Against a target who is familiar with the characteristics of infrared, this would be a significant security consideration if the equipment is not used cautiously. Additionally, a sophisticated target may use equipment, such as a metascope, to actively detect the presence of infrared equipment.

A disadvantage to all NVDs is that they emit considerable light through the eyepiece. This deficiency is overcome by a retractable eyepiece that, when pressed against the face, will open for viewing while shielding the light. When pulled away from the face this eyepiece automatically retracts to close off the emission of light. Night-vision goggles can be worn by a surveillance operator to see and maneuver in the darkness by foot or vehicle. Of course, this is not an effective application when discreet appearance is required.

A final night-vision capability is thermal imaging equipment. This is a passive capability that detects and amplifies radiated heat emitted from animals and machinery, which in the surveillance context equates to the target and his vehicle. Thermal imaging is a particularly effective capability in rural operations where electromagnetic energy can be isolated and detected from miles away.

NVDs are valuable, but they are also expensive. Prior to any purchase, the surveillance team should identify its exact specifications and research which NVD is best suited for its needs. This research should also examine the compatibility of a given NVD with the photographic and video equipment to be used.

Photography and Video Equipment

Unless illumination is favorable, photography and video equipment is significantly limited at night without the assistance of vision-enhancement equipment such as an infrared NVD. Many NVDs are only compatible with certain makes of cameras. Although this problem can usually be overcome with the application of special adaptors, it must be considered in advance. Even with such enhancements, an identification-quality product is difficult.

Infrared film can be used to gain identification-quality photographs when properly used in conjunction with an active device that provides a reflected infrared light source. Low-light photography is possible without vision enhancement, given the appropriate type of film and ideal surrounding illumination. As with the discussion of photographic equipment in Chapter 3, the scope of night photography techniques and applications is too great for this overview.

Binoculars

Binoculars are virtually ineffective at night unless illumination is ideal. Binoculars can be effective during vehicular surveillance follows in some circumstances. Particularly during highway follows, binoculars are helpful in verifying license numbers when used discreetly. Binoculars can be adapted for use with NVDs, but again this is an expensive capability. Specialized binocular NVDs do, however, provide better three-dimensional night viewing detail than monocular NVDs.

Surveillance Vehicles

The surveillance vehicle is the most prominent item of equipment during a night surveillance. The characteristics of night make surveillance vehicles detectable from a greater distance because of their lights. This is the most identifiable signature that a surveillance team will project. Unless the roads are particularly well lit or the surveillance vehicles are following particularly closely, the target will only be able to identify a surveillance vehicle by the signature of its lights. Such a signature can bring a surveillance vehicle to the target's attention initially or make the surveillance vehicle more easily identifiable when observed by the target a second time. Certain precautions can be exercised to take advantage of or lessen the signature at night.

- *Functional Lights.* It is essential that all exterior surveillance vehicle lights are functioning properly. Dim or nonfunctional lights present a signature that is almost impossible to overcome. This includes the proper alignment of lights, which can also project a unique and identifiable signature.
- *Interior Lights.* Disabling the interior lights is the most basic precaution that can be made to a surveillance vehicle in preparation for night surveillance operations. Interior lights can project a great distance at night. By disabling them, an operator can exit or enter the surveillance vehicle without the interior light shining. This avoids drawing attention to a surveillance vehicle that may be otherwise undetectable because of the cover of darkness. Vehicle control panel lights should also be dimmed as appropriate.
- *Adjustable Lights.* Some vehicles are equipped with headlights that can be manually adjusted by a control switch on the control panel. This enables the driver to dim/brighten the lights or adjust their level to alter the signature. By using this control the driver can adjust the lights from one portion of the follow to

another, thus giving the appearance of a different vehicle. If a surveillance vehicle does not come equipped with this feature, the team should consider having it installed.

• *Brake Lights.* Recall that a brake light kill switch can be installed in a surveillance vehicle to conceal the use of brakes when travelling in front of the target. This option is more important at night because the brake lights are more pronounced and can be seen at a much greater distance. Also recall that in most vehicles the brake lights activate when the brake pedal is engaged, even when the ignition is not turned on or the vehicle is not running. When in a box position, an error in this regard will immediately draw the target's attention to the surveillance vehicle as he passes—probably earning the surveillance vehicle enhanced attention from the target.

• *Reverse Lights.* Recall that by employing a reverse-light kill switch in conjunction with a brake light kill switch, a surveillance vehicle can maneuver under the cover of darkness without projecting any light. As with the brake light, the other lights do not have to be activated for the reverse lights to shine when the surveillance vehicle is placed in reverse. It is also important to note that with an automatic transmission vehicle, even when it is not placed in reverse, the reverse lights may flash as the transmission is shifted from the park position to the drive position or, conversely, from drive to reverse.

• *Turn Signals.* The use of turn signals at night will depend on the circumstances of the follow. At night, turn signals stand out significantly and can alert the target to surrounding activity. Also, the detection of turn signals will assist the target in determining vehicles that may be mirroring his movements. For these reasons, judicious use of turn signals is required.

• *License Plate Lights.* The license plate light of a surveillance vehicle is a small factor that makes it more identifiable at night. By disabling the license plate light the overall signature is lowered, as is the possibility of the target identifying the license plate number.

GENERAL NIGHT SURVEILLANCE CONSIDERATIONS

The same basic tactics apply at night as during a daylight surveillance. The most significant difference is the degree of cover involved with a night surveillance operation. This aspect of cover does not only apply to the cover of darkness. Normally, the amount and type of traffic in a given area differs significantly from day to night. In most areas there is significantly less pedestrian and vehicular traffic at night. As the hour of night gets later, the more this traffic tends to decrease.

When preparing for any surveillance operation, the study of the operational area should always anticipate night operations. The character of virtually any area will change significantly as the day turns to night. The primary differences that must be examined are parking availability, traffic density, street illumination, and night spots such as bars. An additional consideration is that police presence is generally intensified at night.

FOOT SURVEILLANCE AT NIGHT

The tactics of a foot surveillance are identical to those employed during the day, with the exception of a few considerations. During a foot surveillance the darkness is of great benefit to the surveillance operator, but it can also be of great benefit to a target who is attempting to elude surveillance. The advantage gained in increased cover from the darkness can be easily negated by limited visibility. The foot operator should dress in a manner that capitalizes on the darkness. Dark colors should be worn, with regard to the rule of dress which warns against extremes.

In many cases, a foot surveillance during darkness will satisfy most individuals' images of the cloak-and-dagger shadow warrior. The operator is not as concerned with looking suspicious to surrounding pedestrians because they may not exist. The operator must use the resources that darkness offers to counter the lack of traffic cover. A team without body communications at night is at a great disadvantage because it is difficult to rely on visual signals that cannot be seen. The Hollywood tactic of lighting a cigarette to signal in darkness is simply not feasible for an extended foot surveillance.

VEHICULAR SURVEILLANCE AT NIGHT

Target Signature
The most important aspect of vehicular surveillance at night

is the rear signature of the target vehicle. During the discussion regarding the stakeout and pickup (Chapter 5), the importance of informing the team of all identifying data regarding the target vehicle was addressed. In night surveillance, identifying data is limited primarily to the signature of the tail and brake lights. Although information regarding the headlights is important, it is the rear of the target that will be keyed on during the follow. Obviously, nonfunctional lights are important to identify because they will assist the surveillance effort immeasurably.

Although information regarding the rear light signature will be transmitted to the team, it is not until the individual operator has the opportunity to observe the rear lights for himself that he is able to develop a mental picture that is essential to future identification. The taillight signature is the most important aspect of the rear signature because it is the one that remains constant. There are many different taillight configurations that are unique to given makes and models of cars. The operator should attempt to develop a mental picture of the lights based on their shape, their width apart, and their shade and brightness.

The shade, brightness, and configuration of the brake lights are critical aspects of the rear signature. It is best to develop a mental picture of how the brake lights project in relation to the taillights. Some vehicles have brake lights built into the taillights so that when the brakes are engaged, the signature shape remains the same while projecting more brightly. Some brake lights are on top of the taillights while others are on the bottom. They can also vary from side to side or consist of a combination of any of these. Some vehicle models have a brake light located in the center base of the rear window. If the brake lights are a different shade of red or a different color altogether than the taillights, this will be of great benefit to the team.

The license plate light is a minor, yet important, aspect of the target's rear signature. Identifying whether it is functional, nonfunctional, bright, or dim assists in differentiating the target vehicle from other vehicles on the road. The brightness, shape, and location of rear turn signals can also assist in identification of the target. The pace of the signal is also helpful in this respect. Most vehicles have turn signals with a standard pace, but there are some models with signals that blink at a faster or slower pace than the standard.

Perhaps the only signature characteristics other than vehicle lights that will assist in the identification of the target at night are the interior and exterior silhouettes. At times, the lights of following or oncoming traffic will project a silhouette of the target vehicle's exterior shape or its interior. Unless either of these is unique, neither can be used solely for identification purposes. They can assist, however, by adding to the overall signature development. The exterior silhouette consists only of the vehicle's shape. The interior silhouette consists of anything visible inside, such as headrests, passengers, and the target himself.

One final note regarding identification of the target vehicle at night. Some "experts" on the art of surveillance advocate the placement of reflective tape on the rear bumper of the target vehicle. This practice is only employed by amateurs with little regard for the security of the operation. The reader should ask himself how long it would take to identify such an addition to his own vehicle. A secure alternative to this practice is the application of infrared reflective tape, which can be very effectively disguised and emits a reflection that is only detectable by infrared devices. There are also chemical compounds that can be rubbed onto a vehicle and detected by specialized sensors. This is a short-term, yet expensive, technology that is only practiced by the world's best-funded surveillance units.

Vehicular Cover Considerations

During the hours of darkness, cover and limited visibility are the primary considerations. Other than these factors, the tactics are identical to those employed during a daylight vehicular surveillance. Generally, darkness provides a cover advantage in urban areas and a cover disadvantage in rural areas. The advantage enjoyed in urban areas assumes some degree of traffic in which the surveillance team can blend. Of course, as the surrounding traffic decreases, so does the degree of cover.

With adequate traffic cover, surveillance vehicles are relatively invisible because it is virtually impossible to distinguish a surveillance vehicle from the surrounding traffic. During the day, the target can identify a surveillance vehicle by such features as make, model, and color. At night, the only distinguishable features are the lights of the surveillance vehicle. Provided that the surveillance vehicle has taken the precautions to ensure that it does not project a readily distinguishable signature, as discussed previously, surrounding traffic will make it invisible. The exception to this rule, of course, is poor tactical execution, which will bring a surveillance vehicle to the target's attention both night and day.

In rural, residential, or even urban areas where there is limited traffic cover, darkness places the surveillance team at a significant disadvantage in respect to remaining discreet. When there are only two sets of headlights on the street and one of them is the target's, there is no place to hide. On dark open roads it is much easier to detect following vehicles because their headlights can be seen at a much greater distance. When the target can see the headlights of both the command and backing vehicles, the security advantage inherent in the exchange of command at an intersection is significantly degraded. When possible, the team should maximize the use of parallels so that the target can be released altogether at a turn and then picked up again by a paralleling surveillance vehicle at a subsequent intersection.

The disadvantages already addressed are compounded on rural roads where there are few parallel roads and following traffic can be seen from a significant distance. In such circumstances, it may be necessary to determine whether the expected results of that portion of the operation are worth the security risk taken by trying to continue the follow—a difficult decision, given the fact that many significant activities take place during the hours of darkness. A surveillance team should seriously consider employing a technical tracking device on the vehicle of a target that develops a pattern of drawing the team into such compromising situations. Aircraft support in monitoring the tracking device is particularly effective.

Tactics of Vehicular Surveillance at Night

Positions in a stakeout box or a standard surveillance box will also differ at night. Area lighting will have a significant impact on surveillance vehicle positioning. Generally, vehicles must be closer in to ensure that the target can be positively identified. Box positions may have to be established directly on the anticipated route of travel rather than adjoining roads. In many circumstances, foot operators will have to be employed as commits for the surveillance vehicles to get close enough for a positive identification of the target.

A pickup on the highway is particularly difficult at night. In some cases, the only way to ensure a successful commit and pick-up is to have a foot operator hidden in a commit position at the shoulder of the highway. Even then the traffic is traveling so fast that positive identification is difficult. Of course, a target with a distinguishable light signature makes the pickup much easier.

As the target breaks the box and the team initiates the pick-up and follow, there are unique factors that must be considered at night. Once again, the driver must keep his foot off the brake pedal. When the target passes a surveillance vehicle that is parked in a box position on the same street, the lighting in many cases will provide the target with a silhouetted view of the surveillance vehicle's interior.

To counter this, operators should use their car seats to prevent their heads and shoulders from projecting a silhouette as the target passes. Safety straps should not be worn until after the target passes because they too can project a silhouette. It is important to note that after the target breaks the box, it is easier for him to detect a surveillance vehicle maneuvering from a box position to follow because of the sudden appearance of headlights. Adequate traffic cover decreases the degree of this risk.

Many of the same characteristics regarding cover discussed previously will also apply to the target during the follow. In dense traffic, it is very difficult to distinguish the target from the other vehicles on the road. This requires that the following distance in such circumstances be much closer than normal. With only the target's taillights to key on, forward traffic can appear as any number of red dots. Unless the target has a very distinguishable taillight signature, it will be difficult to isolate while maneuvering through traffic.

The driver's job is all the more difficult at night because it is his responsibility to maintain visual observation of the target. The navigator is more occupied at night with reading the map by flashlight and consequently is of less help to the driver in observing the target. The driver is also responsible for maneuvering the surveillance vehicle through traffic, but a momentary break in observation as the target maneuvers can result in lost command.

The driver will know that one of the sets of taillights ahead of him is the target but must press in close to determine again exactly which set.

As traffic density decreases, observation becomes much easier. The command vehicle can increase its following distance considerably unless traffic obstacles preclude this. In rural areas the command vehicle can distance itself considerably, but as discussed earlier, the negative aspects of this trade-off outweigh the positive.

The mirroring effect is one aspect of the follow that surveillance vehicles must be sure to avoid during a night surveillance. The movements of following vehicles are more readily identifiable to the target since they can be observed at a greater distance because of headlights. Although the target cannot identify a particular surveillance vehicle, he can still pick up on a mirroring vehicle, thus raising his suspicion.

Surveillance vehicles must also be sure to stagger their distances in situations when the target can see three or more surveillance vehicles to the rear. This is necessary to avoid the *convoy signature*, which is the tendency for surveillance vehicles to position themselves at a standard distance behind each other. The convoy signature can be more readily identified at night because of decreased cover for the team and enhanced visibility for the target because of surveillance vehicle lights. A team signature of three or more surveillance vehicles traveling an equidistance apart is more readily detectable and appears particularly suspicious at night. In addition to the advantages discussed previously, parallels can also be used to avoid exposing multiple surveillance vehicles and to avoid projecting the convoy effect.

In the case of a lost-command drill, a surveillance vehicle may have to pass the target in order to get a positive identification. A positive aspect of this is that there will be less exposure of the surveillance vehicle to the target than would result from such an occurrence during daylight.

LIMITED VISIBILITY SURVEILLANCE OPERATIONS

Conditions of limited visibility require that a surveillance team employ many of the tactics associated with night surveillance operations. There are also additional considerations that the team must realize when conducting operations in such conditions.

Adverse Weather Conditions

Adverse weather conditions such as rain, sleet, or snow can have a significant impact on the conduct of a surveillance operation. Safety considerations are always enhanced in such circumstances.

While in box positions, it is necessary to keep the surveillance vehicle windows clear in order to be able to watch for the target. This is done primarily by the use of windshield wipers and the vehicle defroster. Although necessary, this gives the team's surveillance vehicles a unique signature because they will be among the only vehicles parked along the road with clear windows. This is particularly true in the case of snowfall, but also applies to icy conditions and, a lesser degree, to rainfall.

Not only do these conditions make the surveillance vehicles stand out by their appearance alone, but they will also be the only vehicles parked on the road that can be seen into. When possible, surveillance vehicles should establish box positions that are off the main routes of travel to minimize the possibility of being seen by the target.

Adverse conditions can make it difficult to identify the target by sight or signature. Such conditions are only compounded at night. Adverse conditions normally dictate that following distances be decreased. The effect that the conditions have on the target's visibility will often negate this disadvantage. In the case of a heavy downfall when traveling at high speeds, this can be a greater disadvantage to the surveillance effort. In such circumstances, precipitation generally obstructs vision to the front more than to the rear. This means that while the surveillance vehicles have poor visibility forward, the target may have relatively better vision to the rear. Rear visibility is normally clearest through the side-view mirrors. Wind speed and direction also have an impact on this, although at night the disadvantage is negligible. Such circumstances can be overcome by establishing a command vehicle in front of the target.

Dusk/Dawn Surveillance

Depending on the time of year and the geographical area, the hours of dusk and dawn are those with the heaviest traffic. These are also the times when visibility can be obstructed significantly because of the level of the sun when looking in its direction.

During these hours, surveillance vehicles should attempt to establish box positions in locations where they are not forced to look into the sun to complete their assignment. Additionally, they should attempt to position themselves in a location that forces the target to face the sun when looking in their direction.

The sun can be either an asset or a liability during the follow. When traveling toward the sun, there is poor visibility forward, forcing the team to decrease its following distance. At the same time, although the target's visibility will also be obstructed to the front, it will be relatively clear to the rear. This may result in surveillance vehicles that can be seen clearly by the target. Once again, this can be overcome by establishing a command vehicle in front of the target.

When traveling away from the sun, the team enjoys generally good visibility to the front, while the target's visibility is obstructed to the rear. The only difficulty the team may encounter in this situation is that the sun's reflection off the target's rear window and the windows of the vehicles around it may obstruct the team's visibility.

Surveillance vehicles should use the conditions of dusk to their advantage as a day follow becomes a night surveillance. By keeping their lights off as long as possible without appearing unnatural, surveillance vehicles can use the limited visibility as enhanced cover. At the appropriate time, a surveillance vehicle can turn on its lights after a period of command, thus projecting a completely different signature the next time that surveillance vehicle commands the target. The converse of this concept can be applied as night turns to day.

TAP-RED METHOD

Recall that Chapter 6 discussed the tap-red method of identifying surveillance vehicles. This is a very important tactic to employ in all limited visibility and night surveillance operations.

Even when the operators are familiar with the appearance of all of the team's surveillance vehicles, poor visibility dictates that the operators identify surveillance vehicles by the same method as they do the target—by the taillight signature. This makes recognition difficult, if not impossible, at times. The tap-red method is effective in enabling the team to overcome this limitation.

14

SURVEILLANCE
OPERATION
AFTER-ACTION

Having addressed all the primary methods of surveillance and the associated tactics, this book will conclude with a discussion of the process that ends each surveillance operation: the surveillance operation after-action debriefing.

All periods of a surveillance operation in which the team terminates contact with the target and reassembles will be followed immediately by a debriefing session. The purpose of the team debriefing is to consolidate observations in order to develop a total picture of that period's operation. This also allows the team to record a thorough surveillance report while the details are clear in the operators' minds. The debriefing process is critical to the eventual success of a surveillance operation because it provides an opportunity for the team to conduct target pattern analysis. This enables the team to determine the most effective manner in which to cover the target in subsequent portions of the operation.

Short-term surveillance operations may require only one debriefing at the conclusion of the entire operation. Extended operations will normally consist of many debriefing sessions at the conclusion of each portion of the operation. Extended operations will normally consist of the team covering the target from the time that he leaves his residence in the morning until such time that the team is confident that he has returned to his residence for the night. This may require that the team remain on stakeout at the target's residence until the lights are turned off.

When 24-hour coverage of the target is required, the team will normally operate in two or three shifts to ensure that operators remain rested and alert. This allows each team to debrief at the end of each period of coverage. Twenty-four hour operations for a single team cannot be conducted for long because of fatigue, which results in accidents and poor security practices.

Another disadvantage to such operations is that the team is unable to debrief and learn from each operator's individual observations in a timely manner. One compromise is to employ an around-the-clock observation post of the target's residence while allowing the team to terminate at the end of each day to debrief and rest. This allows the team to determine if the target departs his residence at night after it leaves. When this occurs, the team can adjust its coverage pattern to counter this contingency in the future.

When a surveillance operation, or portion thereof, is terminated, the team will return to a predetermined debriefing location. The debriefing location may be a hotel room or an office. Immediately upon returning to the debriefing location, each team member will inventory individual and surveillance vehicle equipment to ensure that everything is accounted for. This inventory will also identify any equipment that is inoperative and must be exchanged for working equipment.

After the surveillance vehicles and equipment are secured, team members will move to the debriefing location and prepare their surveillance notes. Each operator is responsible for preparing his notes during periods of foot surveillance. Operators will coordinate with any other operators who took notes for them while they where conducting a foot follow. It is important that the operator who made the observations formalize these notes for himself. This ensures that the observations made are attributed to the correct operator—which is very important when presenting the evidence in a criminal proceeding. Lawyers look for such technicalities when defending an otherwise guilty client.

Normally, the navigator of each surveillance vehicle will be responsible for preparing the notes of observations made by the surveillance vehicle crew. In any case, observations attributed to a surveillance vehicle must be prepared by a member of that surveillance vehicle crew, for the same attribution purposes just discussed.

Surveillance notes are thorough dissertations regarding the observations of the target and any other significant information that has a direct impact on the activities of the target. The notations will be in chronological order from the beginning of the operation until the last period of command. Surveillance notes should include the time at which the operator or his surveillance vehicle established command of the target and the time at which command was relinquished. This is done for each period of command. The notes also identify the surveillance vehicle or operator from which command was exchanged at the beginning of the period noted and the surveillance vehicle or operator to which command was passed at the end of the period noted.

When command was established after the target had been unsighted, this is annotated in place of an operator or surveillance vehicle designator. This will also be annotated when the target went unsighted after that period of command. Prepared surveillance worksheets will assist the team in standardizing its notes. An example of a surveillance worksheet is contained in Appendix C.

The entries on surveillance worksheets are limited to the observations of the target and any other significant activity that impacts directly on the investigation. The tactics employed and actions taken by the operators have nothing to do with the activities of the target and should not be noted. Recall that surveillance operator notes should be able to stand as judicial evidence if necessary. It is not in the team's interest to release information regarding the surveillance tactics employed in support of such proceedings.

If a surveillance operation is conducted in support of an investigative agency, a representative of that agency will be present at the debriefing. Normally, the investigative representative will be responsible for preparing the consolidated report. When this is not the case, there should be an individual designated to observe the debriefing and prepare the formal surveillance report. Ideally, this individual will not be actively involved in the surveillance operation because producing a formal report for an active period of coverage is a time-consuming task.

When all the individual operators' notes are completed, the initial portion of the debriefing session will begin. This portion is referred to as the *operational debriefing*. This consists of each operator reading his observations in chronological order. Each period of coverage by an operator or a surveillance vehicle will begin by stating the time that command was established and the operator or surveillance vehicle from which command was exchanged. Again, when command was established after a period of being unsighted, this should be stated.

The operator will identify the target's route of travel and any other pertinent activities of the target that were observed during that period of command. Each period will conclude with the time and location at which command was exchanged and the surveillance vehicle or operator to which command was relinquished. Again, if the target went unsighted to the team after that period of command, this will be noted along with the time and location of lost command. As that operator concludes a briefing on a period of observation, the surveillance vehicle or operator to which command was passed will pick up the debriefing at that point. If the target went unsighted at the conclusion of that period of command, the surveillance vehicle or operator who next noted observations of the target will pick up the debriefing—if in fact the target was observed again.

As with the notes on the surveillance worksheet, during the operational debriefing, operators will not discuss any of the actions they took during the surveillance operation. This only confuses the primary issue—which is to accurately report observations of the target. The tactics employed by the team, both good and bad, are discussed in a subsequent portion of the debriefing session.

The *formal surveillance report* represents the final product of a period of surveillance. If the report fails to accurately capture the results of that period's operation, then the team's efforts may have been without purpose. The surveillance report will consist of three portions: the introduction, the observations section, and the concluding remarks.

The *introduction* to the formal surveillance report will begin by identifying the target of the surveillance and the period of surveillance detailed in the report. The introduction will reference the title and publication date of the map book used by the surveillance team to record its observations. This allows anyone reading the report to follow the information on the map and develop a better picture of the target's travels. Information regarding the objectives and circumstances relating to the surveillance may be included when appropriate.

The *observations section* of the report is based primarily on a chronological compilation of the individual surveillance worksheets. Normally, the first entry to the observations section of the report will begin with the time that the initial stakeout box was established. The identification of periods of stakeout is important because they too provide information even when the target is not under observation. For example, if the target's residence is under stakeout from 6:00 A.M. and the target finally departs at 1:00 P.M., the consumer knows that the target was at home during that seven-hour period. If the target were to return to his residence at 1:00 P.M., the consumer will know that the target was not at home during that seven-hour period and departed prior to 6:00 A.M.

The second entry on the report will be the initial sighting of the target. When the pickup is noted, all subsequent entries to the report will identify the times, routes, and activities observed during the mobile surveillance. The surveillance report should accurately reflect all observations, but should not identify the specific operators or surveillance vehicles that commanded the target at specific times. This information is contained in the individual surveillance worksheets for reference if necessary.

The surveillance report should only contain the specific information that is pertinent to the consumer. Additionally, when the team does not control the dissemination of the report after it is produced, it is important to protect the confidentiality of the team's surveillance tactics and the identities of its members. Again, this is done by leaving the report generic and limiting it to observations of the target and any other information pertinent to the investigation.

The final entry into the observation section of the report will normally include the final stakeout box of the day or that period of surveillance. A successful surveillance will normally conclude with the team following the target to his residence and placing a stakeout box around the location. When the lights go out in the residence or the team determines that the probability of the target departing again is unlikely, it will terminate. Again, it is important to note the length of time that the terminating stakeout was maintained. Other concluding possibilities include the team relinquishing command of the target intentionally or losing command of the target—never to regain it again during that reporting period. In either of these two cases, the final report entry will be the time, location, and circumstances of the last period of command.

Throughout the report it is important to record all periods of lost command accurately. Such entries will include the initial location and length of lost command, as well as the location where command was reestablished—if, in fact, it was. This is important in that it allows the consumer to determine whether there was adequate time for the target to conduct illegal or operational activity during the period of lost command. It also provides the time and general location of where such activity may have occurred. Specific locations checked during periods of lost command will not be included in the observations section of the surveillance report, but may be appropriate in the concluding remarks section.

The *concluding remarks section* of the surveillance report will include any information regarding that period of coverage that impacts on the investigation but was not appropriate for inclusion in the observations section. This will include analytical comments based on the overall patterns of the target's activities. It may also include observations that impact on, or relate to, notations made during previous periods of surveillance. A previous surveillance report should be referenced when this is the case.

Any activity conducted by the target that was indicative of surveillance countermeasures will be thoroughly explained in the remarks section of the report. This is important to note because the use of surveillance countermeasures by the target is a strong indicator that he is, in fact, involved in illegal or operational activity.

As previously addressed, locations that were checked during

periods of lost command may be included in the remarks section of the report. This is appropriate when the information provides the consumer additional insight regarding the target's possible activities during the period of lost command. This may be referred to as *negative information*. By identifying those areas that were checked by the surveillance team in an effort to regain command of the target, it is at least clear where the target did not go during that period.

Any material that can complement the information in the report should be included as *attachments*. Attachments to a report should be directly associated with the report and that specific period of surveillance coverage. When it is essential to the understanding of the surveillance report that the consumer have the correct map book, one may be included as an attachment. Photographs, composite sketches, videotapes, or audio recordings that relate to the observations detailed in the report may be appropriate as attachments. Any other material that was collected and may be used as evidence can be referenced as an attachment to the report.

After the operational debriefing is concluded and the individual preparing the report has been given all the necessary information, the team will conduct the *tactical debriefing portion* of the session. This debriefing will concentrate on the tactics employed by the team during that period of surveillance. The purpose of the tactical debriefing is to discuss what the team did right and wrong during that period of surveillance—as well as ways to improve in the future.

Even the best surveillance teams make mistakes while conducting operations. The mark of a professional team is one that incorporates a process through which to learn from its mistakes to ensure that they are not repeated in the future: The tactical debriefing provides this forum. The high points as well as the low points will be discussed. The debriefing session will range from congratulatory praise to constructive criticism. The team should concentrate on the issues and not personalities to ensure that the session is a positive exercise.

After the tactical debriefing is complete, the team members will register their *exposure states*. Exposure states are the degree of exposure that a given operator had to the target during that period of surveillance. This is normally a subjective judgment on the part of the individual operator. Exposure states will range from one to ten, with one being the lowest degree of exposure. Exposure states assist the surveillance chief in determining the best operator crewing for the next period of the operation.

The surveillance chief will maintain exposure-state records for each operator throughout the operation. When an operator's exposure state reaches the point that he is a risk to security, that operator may need to be replaced or assigned to a low-profile duty, such as an observation post. Exposure states will also be recorded for each of the surveillance vehicles at the end of every period of surveillance.

The debriefing session will conclude with surveillance vehicle crewing, box assignments, and any additional instructions for the next period of surveillance. At the conclusion of the debriefing it is best to get a good night's sleep . . . because the next stakeout is always the most important one.

BREVITY
CODES

ITEM	CODE WORD
AIRPORT	HIVE
AIRPLANE	BEE
ANTISURVEILLANCE	SMOKE
BACKING (able to assume command)	WITH
BANK	WALLET
BAR	LAIR
BEACH/RIVERFRONT	BLUE-LINE
BEACON SIGNAL	BEEP
BINOCULARS	SPECTORS
BRIDGE	LIZARD
BRUSH CONTACT	BOLT
BUS	BEETLE
CAMERA/PICTURE	CHEESE
CAR	ANT
CENTER LANE	TRUE
CHURCH	STAR
CITY	DOMAIN
CONSTRUCTION	TURTLE
CONTACT/MEETING	STRIKE
CONTROL BASE	CASTLE
COMMAND (of the target)	ZERO-ZERO
COMMAND (of the target from in front)	CHEATING
COUNTERSURVEILLANCE	FIRE

DEAD DROP	ASH
DIRECTION OF TRAVEL	FACING
DISGUISE (partial)	SUNTAN
DISGUISE (complete)	SUNBURN
DOWNTOWN	EMPIRE
DROP FOOT OPERATOR(S)	GIVE
EAST	COPPER
EAT	TAP
ELEVATOR	ROCKET
ENTER (go inside)	INFECT
ENTRANCE/EXIT (door or passage)	VEIN
EXCHANGE CONTROL	SLIP
EXIT (leave)	CURE
FEMALE	SOCKET
FLASHLIGHT	AURA
GAS STATION	FEEDER
GAS UP VEHICLE	SIP
GROUND LEVEL	EVEN
HIGHWAY	PYTHON
HIGHWAY OPTION	VIPER
(interchange, exit, entry ramp)	
HOSPITAL	CROSS
HOTEL/MOTEL	CAGE
HOUSE	TRAP
INTERSECTION	COBRA
LEFT LANE	INSIDE
LEVEL ABOVEGROUND	SUN
LEVEL UNDERGROUND	CHINA
LIGHT (traffic, vehicle, residence)	SWORD
LISTENING POST	ANTLER
MALE	PLUG
MILITARY	GREEN
NIGHT-VISION DEVICE	EVIL EYE
NORTH	NICKEL
OBSERVATION POST	MOLE
ON FOOT	FREE
180-DEGREE TURN (U-turn)	FLIP
PARK (recreation area)	FARM
PARKING LOT	KNIFE

PICK UP FOOT OPERATOR(S)	RECEIVE
PEDESTRIAN	RAT
POLICE	STICK
POST OFFICE	PEN
POWER LINE	STRING
PUBLIC LOCATION (in general)	TRAP
RENDEZVOUS	KNOT
RESTAURANT	NEST
REST ROOM	CUP
RIGHT LANE	OUTSIDE
SCHOOL	ZOO
SOUTH	SILVER
SPEED OF TRAVEL	VICTOR
STATION (bus, train, subway)	SNARE
STOPPED (extended period)	DEAD
STORE/SHOP	CAVE
STREET	SNAKE
SUBWAY	WORM
SURVEILLANCE DETECTION	SPARK
TARGET	BETA
TARGET'S INTENTION	INTENDING
TARGET VEHICLE	GAMMA
TARGET'S RESIDENCE	OMEGA
TARGET'S WORKPLACE	EPSILON
TAXI	TERMITE
TELEPHONE	PIDGEON
TELEPHONE TAP	SPLICE
TEMPORARILY STOPPED (traffic light, toll booth)	SNAGGED
TERMINATE OPERATION	CRASH
TRAIN	SPIDER
TRUCK (large commercial)	SLUG
TRUCK (privately owned, pickup or smaller)	BUG
VAN	ROACH
WATER	BLUE
WEST	GOLD

BREVITY

CODE

APPLICATIONS

The brevity codes listed in Appendix A are simply some examples of those which can be used to facilitate radio communications. A well-coordinated surveillance team will use codes that are unique to the originators. Many operations may not be sensitive enough to require the security measures inherent in brevity codes. Despite this fact, brevity codes should be used in all operations because they instill a sense of professionalism that pervades all operational practices.

Any communications traffic analyst who is competent in the field will be able to decipher these or any such series of codes given sufficient intercepted transmissions. This, however, is a time-consuming effort that is primarily characteristic of sophisticated national intelligence agencies. In the event that an operator inadvertently calls an item in the clear, he should not correct the mistake by transmitting the code. This only makes it easier for anyone who may be monitoring the transmissions to determine the code's meaning.

The example codes in Appendix A will be used to

explain operational applications. The code for the target is Beta. Normally there will only be one primary target of a surveillance operation, but this is not always the case. Some operations may begin with more than one target, while others may identify additional targets as progress is made. For this reason it is necessary to number the targets of an operation. If the operation begins with only one primary target, then this individual will be referred to as Beta-1. As any subsequent targets are identified, they will be referred to sequentially as Beta-2, Beta-3, and so on. Operations that begin with more than one target will have the targets designated as Beta-1, Beta-2, and so on based on a prioritization of the targets' importance in satisfying the objectives of the operation.

A target may own more than one vehicle or be a regular passenger in another individual's vehicle. For this reason it is also necessary to sequentially designate target vehicles (Gamma), just as multiple targets are numerically designated. Numbered designations for targets and target vehicles should remain constant as the operation progresses. For example, if an operator informs the team that Beta-2 is driving Gamma-3, the entire team will understand exactly which target and target vehicle the operator is referring to. This same concept of numbering code words also applies to levels above and below ground. For example, if the target is in a building's first level below ground he is China-1; if he is on the third level above ground he is Sun-3.

The number of possible items that the team could identify for coding is unlimited. The team must, however, attempt to limit codes to those that are used regularly. Too many code words are difficult to remember and may only confuse the operation. The codes listed in Appendix A approach the limit of optimal effectiveness, with some room for additional operation-specific codes. There are variations to existing codes that the resourceful team can use to enhance its applications. For example, based on the codes in Appendix A, a shopping mall can be referred to as a Multi-Cave. A fast-food restaurant can be referred to as a Fast-Nest. Codes can also be combined for specification. One example of this is to refer to a police station as a Stick-Snare.

Even with a code for streets and locations, further specification will normally be necessary. This is the most difficult application to brevity codes because the compromise of specific locations through transmissions intercept can be the most revealing about the operation. There are any number of possible streets, street intersections, or stores that an operator may refer to when transmitting the corresponding code. Such locations will normally require more specific identification.

The only method short of transmitting the actual name of the location is to use the phonetic alphabet for identification. For example, a K-Mart store will be identified as the Kilo-Cave. The intersection of Long and Shepherd streets will be identified as the Cobra of Lima-Snake and Sierra-Snake. In areas with a number of streets that begin with the same letter, streets will be further differentiated from each other by using the letters that are necessary for distinction. For example, Brenner Street will be differentiated from Bolton Street by the brevity code Bravo/Romeo-Snake as opposed to Bravo/Oscar-Snake.

The following are examples of brevity code use in operational calls:

Example: The target vehicle is stopped at a red light.
Call: Gamma-1 is snagged at the sword.

Example: The target is walking toward the subway station.
Call: Beta-1 is possibly intending the worm-snare.

Example: The target has entered a bar named Sam's Place as Drake loses command of the target.
Call: Beta-1 has infected the sierra/papa lair; Drake no longer zero-zero.

Example: The target vehicle is traveling in the left lane at a speed of 45 MPH and is the second vehicle ahead of a red pickup truck.
Call: Gamma-1 is inside at victor four-five, two up on the red bug.

Example: A surveillance vehicle is taking pictures of the

target having a personal meet with a white male at the water fountain in the park.

Call: Beta-1 is striking a white-plug at the farm-blue; we have cheese.

Example: The target vehicle has gone straight through the intersection of Market and Northridge streets traveling southwest.

Call: Gamma-1 straight at the cobra of mike-snake and november-snake still facing silver-gold.

Example: The target vehicle conducts a possible surveillance detection maneuver by executing a U-turn in the vicinity of a church.

Call: That's Gamma-1 flipping at the star, possible spark.

Example: The target vehicle has entered the parking lot of an Exxon gas station and parked at the pumps. The target has exited the vehicle and is walking toward a gas pump.

Call: Gamma-1 has infected the knife at the echo-feeder and is dead at a sipper. Beta-1 has cured Gamma-1 and is intending to sip.

Example: Surveillance vehicle Alpha commits the target vehicle north at the shopping center parking exit and is maneuvering for command of the target vehicle.

Call: Gamma-1 is facing nickel from the multi-cave knife vein; Alpha maneuvering for zero-zero.

Example: The target vehicle turns right at an intersection that is dotted on the map by a red dot numbered 12 and is traveling toward an intersection that is dotted on the map by a red dot numbered 25.

Call: That's Gamma-1 right at red one-two facing red two-five.

Example: The lights are off at the target's residence; terminate the operation.

Call: The omega-swords are off; crash.

SURVEILLANCE

WORKSHEET

Operation Name _____ Page ___ of ___ Pages
Date _____ Vehicle _____
Target _____ Operator(s) _____

O/V	Time	Observations	Time	O/V
___	___	_____	___	___
___	___	_____	___	___
___	___	_____	___	___
___	___	_____	___	___
___	___	_____	___	___
___	___	_____	___	___
___	___	_____	___	___
___	___	_____	___	___
___	___	_____	___	___
___	___	_____	___	___
___	___	_____	___	___
___	___	_____	___	___
___	___	_____	___	___
___	___	_____	___	___
___	___	_____	___	___

Note: O/V in the first column refers to the operator or vehicle that passed command of the target to the operator or vehicle noting observations. O/V in the last column refers to the operator or vehicle to which the operator or vehicle noting observations passed command of the target. If the target was unsighted prior to the period of observation noted or went unsighted after the period of observation noted, the entry in the appropriate O/V column will be U/S.